A R

including
- *Life of the Author*
- *List of Characters*
- *Genealogy*
- *A Brief Synopsis*
- *Summaries and Critical Commentaries*
- *Glossaries*
- *Character Analyses*
- *Critical Essays*
- *Suggested Essay Ques...*
- *Related Research Projec...*
- *Selected Bibliography*

by
Rosetta James, B.A.
Teacher of English
New York City

Houghton Mifflin Harcourt
Boston New York

Editor
Gary Carey, M.A., University of Colorado

Consulting Editor
James L. Roberts, Ph.D., Department of
English, University of Nebraska

Production
Wiley Publishing, Inc., Indianapolis Composition
Services

CliffsNotes™ *A Raisin in the Sun*

ISBN: 978-0-8220-1108-8

Printed in the United States of America
DOC 20 19 18
4500799374
For information about permission to reproduce selections from this book,
write to trade.permissions@hmhco.com or to Permissions, Houghton Mifflin
Harcourt Publishing Company, 3 Park Avenue, 19th Floor, New York, New York 10016.

www.hmhco.com

CONTENTS

A RAISIN IN THE SUN
NOTES

A Raisin in the Sun is a play rooted in its own
time that speaks through the years to our own.

Chicago Tribune

LIFE OF THE AUTHOR

Lorraine Vivian Hansberry's *A Raisin in the Sun* exploded onto
the American theater scene on March 11, 1959, with such force that
it garnered for the then-unknown black female playwright the Drama
Circle Critics Award for 1958–59—in spite of such luminous com-
petition as Tennessee Williams' *Sweet Bird of Youth,* Eugene O'Neill's
A Touch of the Poet, and Archibald MacLeish's *J.B.*

Since its Broadway debut, *Raisin* has been translated into over
thirty languages, including the language of the eastern German Sor-
bische minority and has been produced in such culturally diverse
places as China, Czechoslovakia, England, France, and the former
Soviet Union. Its universal appeal defies, in retrospect, some of the
early critics' views of *Raisin* as being simply "a play about Negroes."
Although *Raisin* addresses specific problems of a black family in
Southside Chicago, it also mirrors the very real problems of *all* people.
In an interview with social historian Studs Terkel, Hansberry explains,
". . . in order to create the universal, you must pay very close attention to the specific."

Lorraine Hansberry was born in Chicago on May 19, 1930, the
last of four children born to the independent, politically active,
Republican, and well-to-do Carl and Nannie Perry Hansberry. Hospi-
tals were required at that time to list the racial identities of newborns;
however, upon receiving their daughter's birth certificate, Hansberry's
parents crossed out the word "Negro" and wrote "Black," an act of

minor significance, but certainly a testament to the Afrocentric ideology that the elder Hansberrys bequeathed to their children.

Although 1930 is the year that most Americans associate with the Great Depression, Hansberry's family remained economically solvent through this period. By 1930s standards, the Hansberrys were certainly upper middle class, but by the standards of most Chicago blacks, many of whom lived in abject poverty at this time, they would have been considered "rich."

Hansberry was never comfortable with her "rich girl" status, identifying instead with the "children of the poor." Admiring the feistiness exhibited by these children who were so often left alone, Hansberry often imitated their maturity and independence. They wore housekeys around their necks, symbols of their "latchkey children" status, so Hansberry decided to wear keys around her neck —any keys that she might find, including skate keys —so that she too might be thought of as one of them.

Hansberry never lived in a "Younger" household, although she closely observed such households throughout her childhood. The characters in *Raisin* do not know the middle-class comforts of the Hansberry family; in her plays, Hansberry focuses on the class of black people whom she cared most about, even though her knowledge of these people was, at best, peripheral.

Hansberry's father, Carl, not only established one of the first black savings banks in Chicago, but he was also a successful real estate businessman. Credited with innovating the concept of the "kitchenette," the studio apartment, he was able to maximize all available space, converting a large area into several smaller areas. Always politically active, Carl challenged a Supreme Court decision against integration and won his right to purchase a house in an exclusive Chicago neighborhood where no other blacks lived.

Shortly afterward, Hansberry herself was nearly killed by a brick hurled through a window by angry whites. Hansberry remembers her mother's "standing guard" many times with a loaded gun in order to protect her family from the violence of racism. Such traumatic memories were probably a part of the reason that Hansberry incorporated into her first play the theme of a black family's courageous decision to move into a hostile and new environment.

When Hansberry enrolled at the University of Wisconsin, she had every intention of remaining there for the four years necessary for graduation. However, after two years, her growing interest in the arts took her other places for brief periods. She attended the Art Institute of Chicago, Roosevelt College, the New School of Social Research in New York, and studied art in Guadalajara, Mexico. In New York, she worked on the staff of Paul Robeson's *Freedom* magazine, hung around the theater, read plays and honed her craft. Several critics have noted that Hansberry's artwork, her drawings and sketches, is almost as noteworthy as her writing.

Her father's death at the age of fifty-one touched Hansberry deeply; she often said that it was perhaps her father's constant battle with the forces of racism that hastened his early death. Interestingly, the cause and effect of much of the action in *Raisin* evolves as a consequence of the death of Big Walter, a character whom the audience never sees, although much of the dialogue contains references to him.

Hansberry's own untimely death at the age of thirty-four on January 12, 1965, left a void in American theater and in the circle of black writers. Jean Carey Bond, in an article in *Freedomways* magazine, says of Hansberry: ". . . [her] brief sojourn was, in one of its dimensions, a study in pure style. Born into material comfort, yet baptized in social responsibility; intensely individual in her attitudes and behavior, yet sensitive to the wills and aspirations of a whole people; a lover of life, yet stalked by death—she deliberately fashioned out of these elements an articulate existence of artistic and political commitment, seasoned with that missionary devotion which often intensifies the labors of the mortally ill . . ."

Hansberry left behind three unfinished plays and an unfinished semi-autobiographical novel.

HANSBERRY'S MAJOR WORKS

WRITINGS

The Movement: A Documentary of a Struggle for Equality, (a collection of photographs), Simon & Schuster, 1964, introduction by Ronald Segal. Penguin, 1965.

To Be Young, Gifted, and Black: Lorraine Hansberry in Her Own Words, self-illustrated, adapted by Robert Nemiroff, introduction by James Baldwin. Prentice-Hall, 1969.

PLAYS

A Raisin in the Sun: A Drama in Three Acts (first produced in New York City at the Ethel Barrymore Theatre, March 11, 1959) Random House, 1959.

A Raisin in the Sun (screenplay), released by Columbia, 1960.

The Sign in Sidney Brustein's Window: A Drama in Three Acts (first produced in New York City at the Longacre Theatre, October 15, 1964) Random House, 1965.

Les Blancs (first produced in New York City at the Longacre Theatre. November 15, 1970) Samuel French, 1972.

The Collected Last Plays of Lorraine Hansberry, containing *The Drinking Gourd, What Use Are Flowers?,* and *Les Blancs,* introduction by Julius Lester. Random House, 1972; New American Library, 1987.

RECORDINGS

Lorraine Hansberry Speaks Out, Caedmon, 1972.

LIST OF CHARACTERS

Ruth Younger

The thirtyish wife of Walter Lee Younger and the mother of Travis, their ten-year-old son. Ruth acts as peacemaker in most of the explosive family situations. Very low-key, Ruth reveals her strongest emotions only when she learns of the possibility of their moving to a better neighborhood.

Travis Younger

The ten-year-old son of Walter and Ruth Younger. Living in a household with three generations in conflict, Travis skillfully plays each adult against the other and is, as a result, somewhat "spoiled." In spite of this, he is a likeable child.

Walter Lee Younger

In his middle thirties, he is the husband of Ruth, father of Travis, brother of Beneatha, and son of Lena (Mama) Younger. Walter works as a chauffeur and drinks a bit too much at times. When he discovers that his mother will receive a $10,000 check from his father's insurance, he becomes obsessed with his dreams of a business venture which will give him financial independence and, in his mind, will make him a more valuable human being.

Beneatha Younger

The twentyish sister of Walter Lee and the daughter of Lena Younger. She is a college student planning to go to medical school. The only family member privileged to have the opportunity for a higher education, she is sometimes a little overbearing in the pride she takes in being an "intellectual."

Lena Younger (Mama)

The mother of Walter Lee and Beneatha, mother-in-law of Ruth, and grandmother of Travis. Lena's (Mama's) every action is borne out of her abiding love for her family, her deep religious convictions, and her strong will that is surpassed only by her compassion. Mama's selfless spirit is shown in her plans to use her $10,000 insurance check for the good of her family, part of which includes plans to purchase a house in a middle-class white neighborhood.

Joseph Asagai

An African college student from Nigeria, Asagai is one of Beneatha's suitors. Mannerly, good looking and personable, he is well liked by all members of the Younger household.

George Murchison

Beneatha's other boyfriend, he too is a college student. His wealthy background alienates him from the poverty of the Youngers.

Easily impressed, Ruth is the only member of the Younger household who naively overlooks George's offensive snobbishness.

Mrs. Johnson

Brash and abrasive neighbor of the Youngers, she insensitively points out to the Youngers all the negative repercussions that await them should they decide to move into the white neighborhood.

Karl Lindner

A weak and ineffectual middle-aged white man, Lindner is the spokesman for the white community into which the Youngers plan to move. He has been sent to persuade the Youngers not to move into the white neighborhood. In fact, he has been authorized by the white community to offer the Youngers a monetary incentive *not* to move in.

Bobo

The somewhat dimwitted friend of Walter Lee who, along with another friend, Willy, plans to invest in Walter Lee's business scheme.

Two Moving Men

Having no speaking parts, they enter at the end of the play to help the Youngers move to their new neighborhood.

Walter Younger

The husband of Lena Younger, father of Walter Lee and Beneatha, and grandfather of Travis. His death before the action of Act I provides the insurance money that will change the lives of the Younger family.

Willy

The unscrupulous "friend" of Walter Lee and Bobo who absconds with all the money for the prospective business venture. Although the audience never meets him, Willy's character is assessed through the dialogue of others.

A Raisin in the Sun Genealogy

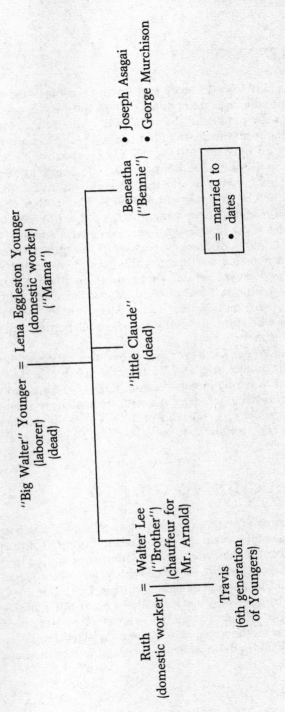

"Big Walter" Younger = Lena Eggleston Younger
(laborer)   (domestic worker)
(dead)   ("Mama")

Walter Lee
("Brother")
(chauffeur for
Mr. Arnold)

Ruth =
(domestic worker)

Travis
(6th generation
of Youngers)

"little Claude"
(dead)

Beneatha
("Bennie")

• Joseph Asagai
• George Murchison

= married to
• dates

A BRIEF SYNOPSIS

This play tells the story of a lower-class black family's struggle to gain middle-class acceptance. When the play opens, Mama, the sixty-year-old mother of the family, is waiting for a $10,000 insurance check from the death of her husband, and the drama will focus primarily on how the $10,000 should be spent.

The son, Walter Lee Younger, is so desperate to be a better provider for his growing family that he wants to invest the entire sum in a liquor store with two of his friends. The mother objects mainly for ethical reasons; she is vehemently opposed to the idea of selling liquor. Minor conflicts erupt over their disagreements.

When Mama decides to use part of the money as a down payment on a house in a white neighborhood, her conflict with Walter escalates and causes her deep anguish. In an attempt to make things right between herself and her son, Mama entrusts Walter Lee with the rest of the money. He immediately invests it secretly in his liquor store scheme, believing that he will perhaps quadruple his initial investment.

One of Walter Lee's prospective business partners, however, runs off with the money, a loss which tests the spiritual and psychological mettle of each family member. After much wavering and vacillating, the Youngers decide to continue with their plans to move —in spite of their financial reversals and in spite of their having been warned by a weak representative of the white neighborhood that blacks are not welcome.

INTRODUCTION TO THE PLAY

Hansberry's recognition of the close relationship between art and propaganda is the reason she chose the environment of the powerless as a backdrop for her work about American culture. Her objective was to be a spokesperson for those who, prior to *Raisin,* had no voice. The thought that anyone outside of the black community would care about the struggles of a black family in Southside Chicago, prior to the opening of *Raisin,* was all but preposterous. Not only did Hansberry choose as the voice of her theme a black family (and a *poor* black family, at that), but she also threaded information about Africa throughout the fabric of her play, mainly through her most stable character, Asagai, Beneatha's suitor from Nigeria.

Through Asagai (and sometimes through Beneatha), the audience gains valuable insight into African history, politics, art, and philosophy. Even the character of George Murchison glorifies, by default, the ancient African civilizations when he derisively mentions "the African past," "the Great West African Heritage," "the great Ashanti empires," "the great Songhay civilizations," "the great sculpture of Bénin," and "poetry in the Bantu." Although George is being facetious, still he uses adjectives that praise and laud the accomplishments of a continent with which many theatergoers, at the time of the opening of *Raisin,* were extremely unfamiliar.

To structure her drama, Hansberry utilizes the **traditional classic** European dramatic forms: *Raisin* is divided into three conventional acts with their distinct scenes. Yet, Hansberry employs techniques of the **absurdist** drama —particularly in the scene in which a drunken Walter Lee walks in on Beneatha's African dancing and is able to immediately summon a memory which psychically connects him with an African past that his character, in reality, would not have known. Walter Lee is able to sing and dance and chant as though he had studied African culture.

Hansberry's skillful use of this momentary absurdity makes Walter's performance seem absolutely plausible to her audience. Note also in this work that Hansberry refers to an ancient Greek **mythological** titan, Prometheus, then makes a reference to an icon of the American entertainment world, Pearl Bailey, and then a reference to Jomo Kenyatta, a major African scholar and politician, yet there is no loss of continuity because the audience is able to immediately perceive the connection.

SUMMARIES AND CRITICAL COMMENTARIES

ACT I—SCENE 1

Summary

The Younger family lives in a cramped, "furniture crowded" apartment that is clearly too small for its five occupants in one of the poorer sections of Southside Chicago. Walter Lee wants to invest

Mama's $10,000 insurance check in a liquor store venture with two of his friends. Because of her religious convictions against liquor drinking, Mama is uninterested in Walter's dream of getting rich quickly with this scheme. Ruth, Walter's wife, is so exhausted from overwork that she too is unsympathetic to Walter's obsession with the money. Mama makes it clear that part of the check will go toward Beneatha's education in medical school. At the beginning of the play, money is the focal point of everyone's conversation, leading to arguments and creating a mood of conflict. Walter leaves for his chauffeur's job, and Travis leaves for school. Ruth prepares for her job as a cleaning woman as Mama reprimands Beneatha about her fresh talk. At the end of the scene, Mama discovers that Ruth has fainted and fallen to the floor.

Commentary

Lorraine Hansberry's debt to Richard Wright can be noted in the similarities between Hansberry's Walter Lee and Wright's Bigger Thomas. Hansberry's play even opens with the ringing of an alarm clock, as does *Native Son*. *Raisin* opens on a Friday morning as everyone is getting ready to leave the apartment for their respective obligations: Walter Lee and Ruth have to go to their jobs; Travis and Beneatha have to go to school.

When the alarm clock rings, Ruth is the first one up, as though it is her responsibility to make certain that everyone else gets up and ready for the day ahead. Ruth is weary and overworked, a parallel to the apartment, which is worn out and weary in appearance from "accommodating the living of too many people for too many years." The apartment consists of only two full-sized rooms, the larger one serving as both the living room and the kitchen. Travis sleeps on the living room couch. Ruth and Walter Lee's bedroom is actually a small alcove just off the kitchen, originally intended to be a "breakfast room" for a smaller, wealthier family. Mama and Beneatha share the only actual bedroom of this "apartment." The single bathroom is shared by their neighbors, the Johnsons, who apparently have a similar "apartment."

Ruth appears to be annoyed with Walter, although she does not openly admit it. At first, Walter seems too preoccupied with thoughts about the insurance check to consider what might be troubling Ruth. Their conversation revolves around money and the lack thereof; even young Travis is concerned with money, as he asks, "Check coming tomorrow . . . ?, and tells Ruth that his teacher asked the students to bring fifty cents to school today.

Walter admonishes Ruth for telling Travis that they cannot give him fifty cents, and we are immediately more sympathetic to Walter than to Ruth, for their dialogue is reminiscent of the mother in Kathryn Forbes' play *I Remember Mama,* who insists that children not be told when there is no money because it makes them worry. Forbes' play revolves around a mother's lie to her children about a nonexistent bank account. In *Raisin,* not only does Walter give Travis the fifty cents that he has requested, but Walter throws in an additional fifty cents — none of which he can afford. Travis never knows that Walter cannot afford to give him the money. After Travis leaves, Walter eats his breakfast; then, ready to leave for work, he tells Ruth that he needs carfare to get to work.

In this scene, note that Ruth's annoyance with Walter is evident in the manner in which she chooses to wake him up. She is "out of sorts" about something that is not yet clear, although it appears to have something to do with Walter. She asks Walter what kind of eggs he wants, yet she ignores his request for "not scrambled" and scrambles the eggs anyway.

The characters are so real in this scene that it is difficult to take anyone's side. When Walter expresses a desire to have the insurance money in order to invest in a business venture, he makes sense — even in his argument with Beneatha. Beneatha is a college student who will require a considerable amount of money for medical school, but the reader wonders if Beneatha's dream for her future is more important than Walter's. As far as we can tell, Beneatha has been given every opportunity to develop her potential. Why not the same for Walter Lee, who makes a strong point when he says of Big Walter (whose death has provided the $10,000): *"He was my father, too!"*

One of the key focuses in this scene is Mama's concern for her family; it especially emphasizes her all-consuming love for her grandson, Travis, as she makes excuses for the careless way in which he made his bed, while re-doing it correctly for him. This scene also shows Mama's strength as head of her household. When Beneatha displays her belligerence and "college girl" arrogance by loudly and emphatically stating that there is no God, Mama slaps her, forcing Beneatha to state aloud, "In my mother's house there is still God."

Later, Mama acknowledges her awareness of a generational rift that appears to be growing between herself and her children.

When the scene ends, we are left with the feeling that everyone else is so self-absorbed that it is only Mama who senses immediately that something seems to be wrong with Ruth, although Ruth insists that she has to go to work regardless of how she feels. However, Ruth's fainting at the end of this scene is proof that she really does require medical attention.

_____

(Here and in the following chapters, difficult allusions, words and phrases are explained, as are these below.)

- **crocheted doilies** The totally bare, classic-line furniture of the fifties contrasted starkly with the furniture of the forties. In the forties, it was customary to place *crocheted doilies* on the arms and head rests of an overstuffed living room sofa and two sofa chairs, which were usually already covered with slipcovers. This was done in an effort to protect the furniture and to hide worn places; the country was just coming out of the Great Depression and great value was placed on one's possessions — especially if a family was poor. Having "forties furniture" in the fifties is a clear indication of poverty.

- **Chicago's Southside** the area in Chicago in which many blacks live; referred to as "the ghetto," the poor neighborhood of Chicago.

- **make down bed** a couch that does not convert into an actual bed but is made up at night with a bed covering and pillow to look like a bed.

- **a settled woman** a woman who looks older than her actual years mainly because she has resigned herself to her "lot in life."

- **always in his voice there is a quality of indictment** a description of Walter, who has grown increasingly accusatory about the bleakness of his financial future.

- **affecting tea party interest** because Ruth is overwhelmed by her own concerns (mainly, that she might be pregnant), she becomes annoyed and therefore sarcastic when Walter tries to involve her in his conversation about the lives of wealthy whites. Ruth "affects" or "puts on" a *tea party* voice, purposely sounding pretentious in order to make Walter leave her alone.

- **slubborness** Ruth refers to Travis' habits as being "slubborn" when she really means both "sloppy" and "stubborn." Because of Ruth's lack of formal education, she is not aware (but the audience is) that this is not a real word.

- **not a single penny for no caps** a popular children's toy in the fifties, especially for little boys, was the "cap pistol" or "cap gun," into which "caps" were placed, producing the sound of a miniature firecracker, making the children feel as though they were actually firing a real pistol. Ruth admonishes Travis even before he asks for money for caps, revealing her negative feelings about caps and cap guns.

- **fly-by-night proposition** a reference to Walter Lee's idea for a business, a proposition that appears to his family to be risky, irresponsible, and unreliable.

- **I don't want that on my ledger** a religious woman, Mama is referring to the book of checks and balances that she believes is kept in Heaven, listing all the good and all the bad that a person does while on earth.

- **my girl didn't come in today** Ruth works as a domestic, a cleaning woman, for wealthy whites who have traditionally referred to these cleaning women as "girls" —a term that the domestics found degrading but never complained openly about for fear of losing their jobs. Even though the cleaning woman was around thirty, as Ruth is, she was still called a "girl." Even Mama's being in her sixties does not mean that she would not also be referred to as the cleaning "girl" or just "the girl," most especially when the white employers were talking among themselves.

- **if the salt loses its savor** when Ruth says that Beneatha is fresh —and then adds that Beneatha is as "fresh as salt," Beneatha counters with a pedantic response, a phrase from the Bible, just to show off her knowledge. Beneatha uses the quote with some pretentiousness to press the point that she knows the Bible from an intellectual point of view but that she does not believe in its religious messages. The phrase used by Beneatha is taken from three places in the Bible:

  Matthew 5:13 "Ye are the salt of the earth: but if the salt have lost his savour wherewith shall it be salted? It is thenceforth good for nothing, but to be cast out, and to be trodden under foot of men."

  Mark 9:50 "Salt is good: but if the salt have lost its saltness, wherewith will ye season it? Have salt in yourselves, and have peace one with another."

  Luke 14:34-35 "Salt is good: but if the salt have lost his savour, wherewith shall it be seasoned? It is neither for the land, nor yet for the dunghill, but men cast it out. He that hath ears to hear, let him hear."

ACT I—SCENE 2

Summary

The following morning, Saturday, is the day that the check is expected to arrive. Beneatha and Mama are busy doing weekend housecleaning when Ruth comes in, announcing sadly that she is pregnant. Mama is upset when she realizes that Ruth is contemplating an abortion. Joseph Asagai brings Beneatha a gift of African records and some Nigerian robes. After he leaves, Travis brings in the insurance check from the mailbox, and Walter seizes this opportunity to discuss his business plans again. Mama, however, ignores Walter in the same way that Walter earlier ignored Ruth's attempts to tell him about her pregnancy. Mama eventually has to be the one to tell him about Ruth's dilemma and is surprised that his desire for the money overshadows his concern for both Ruth and for his unborn child.

Commentary

This scene focuses on the fierce Younger pride that Mama is constantly trying to instill in her children. Although they are poor — still, their house is clean; although the furniture is old, there is still the ritualistic weekly polishing. When Asagai telephones for permission to drop by, Beneatha consents reluctantly because she knows that her mother would not want company to see the house in disarray.

This scene emphasizes the clash of cultures between the American-born black and the African. It is clear that Beneatha and Asagai love each other, but there are hints of philosophical disagreement. Asagai teases Beneatha for straightening her hair in order to conform to the European or Hollywood standard of beauty. Asagai is also more serious about their relationship than Beneatha is and appears not to fully understand or accept Beneatha's "liberated college woman's attitude." Although Asagai is not offensively sexist, perhaps due to his Western education and worldly sophistication, still his views are traditionally African, circa 1959, and, therefore, somewhat chauvinistic.

Hansberry uses this scene to express her dissatisfaction with most people's distorted perceptions about Africa. When the play opened in 1959, all that most people knew about Africa was via the broadcasts from the various colonial rulers and/or the Hollywood messages contained in Tarzan movies. Before Asagai's arrival at the Younger apartment, Beneatha sternly admonishes her mother not to say anything embarrassingly naive or patronizing about Africa. Beneatha gives Mama some facts about Africa which Mama later parrots for Asagai's acceptance and Beneatha's approval. This scene significantly dramatizes the lack of understanding between parent and child. An intellectual gap, however, also compounds the generational difference between Mama and her daughter Beneatha. Mama tries so hard to impress Beneatha's Nigerian friend that her remarks are almost comical, clearly not her intent.

Beneatha wants to know everything about Africa and is more than pleased when Asagai gives her authentic Nigerian robes, along with some recordings of African music. After Asagai leaves, Beneatha tries on her new identity. Ruth comes into the room just as Travis goes downstairs to get the mail. When Walter enters and begins talking about his plans for the money, everyone ignores him so he resorts to shouting: "WILL SOMEBODY PLEASE LISTEN TO ME TODAY?"

Even if Walter's ideas were unacceptable and offensive, someone in his family should have taken the time to listen. The frustration Walter Lee exhibits in this scene is recognizable by everyone who has ever felt ignored in spite of loud cries to be heard. It is difficult in such a crowded atmosphere as the Younger household for one person to be singled out and heard. The Youngers do not mean to ignore Walter Lee — and are not totally aware that they are doing so. They are simply caught up in the excitement of the moment — the receipt of the check.

The original production of this play, as well as the original movie screenplay, does not contain the incident involving Travis' chasing a huge rat while he is downstairs playing with his friends in the street. The scene is included in the PBS presentation, however. Hansberry wrote the "rat scene" to dramatically point out the graphic terrors that daily confront the children of the poor and also to show that these children must learn to incorporate such horrific realities into their playtime activities.

• **behind the bureau** a bureau is a piece of furniture that was usually kept in the bedroom and used for storing clothing. A dresser, in contrast, is a short piece of bedroom furniture that has drawer space, a large mirror, and a small stool or chair where one might sit in order to put on makeup. The bureau is the taller piece of bedroom furniture, containing only drawer space for clothing. Objects placed on top of the bureau often landed behind it which, because of its size and weight, was often a difficult piece of furniture to move.

- **Hay-lo** Beneatha answers the telephone with this greeting, a combination of "Hey" and "Hello."

- **Nigeria** The most populated nation in Africa with more than 250 different ethnic groups. The four major groups are the Hausa and Falani people in the north, the Yoruba people in the southwest and the Ibo people in the southeast. Nigeria was ruled by the Portuguese at the end of the fifteenth century, followed by the Dutch, the Danes, the Spaniards, and the Swedes. At the beginning of the eighteenth century, the British gained control over the slave trade there. Nigeria finally became independent and a member of the British Commonwealth of Nations, and in 1963, it became a republic. Open hostility, however, between the numerous rival factions within the country bred chaos, with several attempts to overthrow the government, civil war, and finally mass starvation. Despite its harrowing past, Nigeria has become a leader in literature, art, music, and craftsmanship.

- **They need more salvation from the British and the French** Beneatha says this to Mama as she attempts to "educate" her mother to what Beneatha feels are political realities. She knows that Mama believes in giving money to her church for the missionary work, but the Africans, she says, "need more salvation from the British and the French," who were the dominant colonial rulers at that time.

- **We've all got acute ghetto-itis** Beneatha says this when Asagai drops by to visit, immediately after the Younger family has had a depressing conversation about their financial station in life and Ruth's possible pregnancy. Beneatha refers to the "ghetto" in which they live as though it brings with it a disease that she calls "ghetto-itis."

- **Mr. Asagai, I am looking for my *identity*** Asagai repeats Beneatha's words to her, poking fun at her desperation to connect with her African heritage. Beneatha made this statement to Asagai when they first met, a remark he had found amusing.

- **One for Whom Bread — Food — Is Not Enough** Asagai gives Beneatha the Nigerian name "Alaiyo," which he translates roughly as: "One for whom bread — food — is not enough," meaning that his perception of Beneatha is that she is a totally developed person, both intellectually and spiritually and that she demands answers to *all* of life's questions. Merely going through the motions of life is not enough for a person like Beneatha; she has to question every philosophy for herself. She is, to Asagai, a person for whom "bread —food —is not enough."

- **You don't have to ride to work on the back of nobody's street-car** Prior to the civil rights movement, which reached its peak in the sixties, segregated facilities, separating whites from blacks, were common in the south, where "Jim Crow" laws made it legal. (Even in the northern cities, vestiges of segregation were apparent.) In the south, whites rode in the front of buses, blacks in the back. An interesting aspect of this particular "Jim Crow" law was that a black person might be permitted to sit in the front of the bus if there were no white person on the bus who needed that seat. If a white person boarded the bus and a black person was seated in the front, the black person knew, almost instinctively, that he had to get up, in deference to the white person who needed that seat.

During the thirties and forties, the mass exodus of blacks from the south to the northern cities was an attempt to flee segregation injustices, including being forced to ride at the back of buses. Not until Rosa Parks dramatically refused to sit at the back of a bus in Montgomery, Alabama, in 1954, an act which accelerated the civil rights movement, did most blacks in the south even think about the absurdity of the "Jim Crow" laws.

Mama's generation worked hard so that their children could have a "better life," which, to her, meant a life without segregation. To those of Mama's generation, it should have been enough that Walter Lee's generation can ride at the front of a bus. Mama cannot understand why Walter Lee wants *more* from life than to sit anywhere he wants on public transportation.

Walter, in contrast, and others of his generation, take that particular "freedom" for granted. Walter wants the larger freedom of being totally independent of everyone; he wants to be able to earn his living without having a "boss"; more important, he wants to be able to generate his own income without being dependent on a salary as a chauffeur. In short, Walter is questioning the reasons he cannot live the way his bosses live. When he asks why his wife cannot wear pearls, he is asking why he *has* to resign himself to poverty, being ever grateful that he no longer has to ride at the back of a bus. To Mama, that particular measure of equality is enough; to Walter, it is an outrage.

ACT II —SCENE 1

Summary

Later that Saturday, dressed in her new Nigerian robes and headdress, Beneatha dances to African music while simultaneously giving

Ruth an impromptu lesson in its significance. Walter comes in, after having had a few too many drinks, and joins in Beneatha's ritualistic dance. The doorbell rings suddenly, and George Murchison arrives for his theater date with Beneatha. He gets into a heated debate with her over the history and heritage of black people, all of which he belittles as insignificant, and then he antagonizes Walter by dismissing Walter's attempts to discuss his "big" business plans with him.

After George's exit, Walter Lee and Ruth reminisce about their early days together and contrast their early dreams and warm feelings for one another, compared to now, when they seem to be slipping away from one another. Mama returns unexpectedly and announces to Travis especially — and also to Walter and Ruth — that she has put a hefty down payment on a house in an all-white neighborhood. Ruth can not contain her happiness at the thought of their finally being able to move out of the overcrowded apartment. Walter, however, is crushed by Mama's news; to him, Mama has "butchered his dream."

Commentary

This scene emphasizes Beneatha's naivete about African culture, for although she is wearing the Nigerian robe and headdress, she is "fanning herself with an ornate oriental fan" and inadvertently appears more Asian than African. Also, Ruth reveals her lack of knowledge about things African as she questions Beneatha about the Nigerian outfit and dance. Walter's sudden intrusion into the dance is comical on the surface, but on a deeper level, Walter Lee appears somewhat tragic as he attempts to recapture his lost African past.

Here, Hansberry is able to make several points:

(1) Even though Walter knows little about Africa, he immediately falls into step with the ritualistic dance and chants as though a psychic memory serves him.

(2) Most blacks wanting to gain acceptance and possible wealth would have to throw off their African past and assimilate, as George has done, which includes deriding and belittling their African culture.

(3) Although Asagai has received a Western-style education, as George Murchison has, Asagai does not have a problem of

identity. He knows who he is because he *is* African. Murchison, on the other hand, knows nothing of his African past, despises the little he knows of his heritage and, therefore, hates himself. His self-hatred manifests itself in his contemptuous attitude toward other blacks, especially toward less wealthy and less educated blacks, like Walter.

(4) Both Beneatha and George Murchison seem to be pedants, showing off their learning, but George is offensive when he flaunts his knowledge in order to *insult* and *degrade* others. Although George suspects that Ruth has never been to the theater — and certainly not a theater in another state — he insists on giving Ruth unnecessary information about the difference between curtain times in Chicago and New York's theaters.

George calls Walter Lee "Prometheus" in order to subtly insult Walter, but mainly to point out Walter's lack of learning. This scene clearly reveals Walter Lee's lack of formal education because Walter assumes that George has simply invented the name "Prometheus" to annoy him.

(5) In addition, this scene illustrates how difficult it is to be Walter Lee Younger without being bitter. When George Murchison refers to Walter Lee as "bitter," Walter Lee agrees that he's bitter; Walter also wonders how George can be content having to live as a second-class citizen — in spite of his wealth — and not be bitter himself.

(6) Hansberry also uses this scene in order to validate the natural hairstyle (unstraightened hair on black women) — a very new concept in 1959 — and even considered somewhat radical when this play opened, but a hairstyle which became popular in the late sixties as the "Afro" hairstyle. When Beneatha reenters, dressed for her date with George, she is wearing a natural hairstyle. Ultra-conservative George surprises everyone with his praise of Beneatha's new look; however, his attitude is patronizing and condescending, as though she requires his approval.

(7) Finally, in this scene, Hansberry makes an emphatic statement about integration. Ruth is apprehensive, almost fright-

ened, when she hears that the new house is located in the all-white neighborhood of Clybourne Park. But Mama explains that a comparable house in a black neighborhood would cost twice as much. Mama is not moving to Clybourne Park because she wants to *integrate* a neighborhood; instead, she simply wants the best deal for her money. This scene is often the most misinterpreted of all the scenes in the play.

- **fanning herself ... mistakenly more like Butterfly than any Nigerian** This stage direction refers to Beneatha's exuberance after receiving the gift of the Nigerian robes and headdress from Asagai. Because Beneatha is not accustomed to African dress, she does not "wear" it properly. Although she is dressed like a Nigerian woman, she begins to dramatically fan herself in order to accentuate her outfit, but she inadvertently loses the African look and appears more Asian, looking as though she's Madame Butterfly instead of African royalty.

- **Ethiopia** References to Ethiopia can be found in the Bible and in the writings of Herodotus and Homer. For much of its history, Ethiopia was known as Abyssinia. Although it is documented that as early as the first century B.C. some Middle Eastern traders settled there, Ethiopian history cites Queen Makeda of Ethiopia and King Solomon as being the parents of Menelik I who, during his reign, founded the kingdom of Ethiopia in 10 B.C. Queen Makeda was known by many names: "Bilquis" to the ancient Moslems, "Black Minerva" and "Ethiopian Diana" to the Greeks, "Queen of Sheba" to King Solomon, and to her own people, she was "Makeda, the beautiful."

  Queen Makeda was so impressed with the wisdom of King Solomon that she visited him in Jerusalem, adopted his religion of Judaism and, upon the birth of their first child, who was a male, she crowned this child King of Ethiopia, an act which united the two nations. She named this child Ibn-al-Hakim, which means "son of the wise man," but he was popularly known as Menelik.

  In 1889, Sahaba Mariem rose to power in Ethiopia, ascended the throne and changed his name to Menelik II, signifying blood ties to Menelik, Makeda's son. Menelik II initiated the modern age of Ethiopian development by defeating the Italians, who were trying to establish a protectorate over Ethiopia. Under his reign, roads were constructed, formal education and social services were instituted, and electricity was introduced. Menelik II is also responsible for relocating the capital at Addis Ababa and for modernizing the operation of government.

The most dominant figure in recent Ethiopian history is Haile Selassie I, also known as "the Conquering Lion of the Tribe of Judah, the Elect of God, and King of Kings." He was crowned Emperor in 1930. Five years later, in 1935, after Selassie had offered his people a written constitution and educational and administrative reforms, Mussolini invaded Ethiopia and occupied the country until 1941, when the British forced the Italians out, and Haile Selassie returned to his throne. During the following decades, Haile Selassie became a symbol of leadership to other African nations that eventually would demand their independence. The founding of the Organization of African Unity, under Haile Selassie, and the headquartering of the OAU in Addis Ababa attests to the respect that Selassie received from the people of Africa.

- **The lion is waking** This phrase refers to all of the African countries that were beginning to demand their independence of colonial rule. The reference was somewhat unsettling to colonial rulers of that day because of the suggested imagery of the fates of those caught in the presence of an awakening, ferocious lion. This phrase also refers to the Lion of Judah.

- **Owimoweh** "Owimoweh" is the title of an African chant, referring to the waking of the lion. Contained in an early sixties song, subtitled "The Lion Sleeps Tonight," the word was made popular by Pete Seeger and the Weavers.

- **a descendant of Chaka** Chaka, also known as Shaka, or Shaka Zulu, was an early nineteenth century African warrior-king who implemented warfare techniques and weaponry which have been studied and adopted by military leaders and personnel worldwide ever since Shaka's time. Shaka Zulu incorporated into his own army the warriors from defeated tribes; he also established military towns in order to ensure that his armies were well provided for and excellently trained. Shaka Zulu initiated the idea of complex battle formations in order to outflank and confuse his enemies, not unlike those strategies used in football formations. In addition, Shaka Zulu revolutionized the existing Zulu weaponry by designing a short handled stabbing spear, known as the "assegai." To this day, the name Shaka Zulu garners high praise in military circles and commands great respect.

  Hansberry's description of Walter as he chants to the African music with Beneatha includes a reference to Shaka Zulu, or Chaka: "On the table, very far gone, his eyes pure glass sheets. He sees what we cannot, that he is a leader of his people, a great chief, a descendant of Chaka, and that the hour to march has come . . ."

- **Ashanti** Beneatha's reference to the Ashanti people, along with George Murchison's references to the **Songhay Empire, Benin,** and the **Bantu** language show that Hansberry herself had some knowledge of the African continent and its culture. Because her uncle, Leo Hansberry, was a professor of African history at Howard University and, perhaps, because one of his students was Kwame Nkrumah, who led **Ghana** to independence, Hansberry's major geographical focus here appears to be on the history of **Ghana**, known prior to its independence as "The Gold Coast."

The **Ashanti**, originally a part of present-day **Ghana**, were people within the **Ghana Empire** whose ascendancy was based on the iron and gold found within this wealthy country. By 1180, however, a group of rival tribes united as the nation of **Mali**, ravaged **Ghana**, and put an end to its empire.

The new **Mali Empire**, larger and more wealthy that the former empire of **Ghana**, reached from the Atlantic Ocean to the Niger River and north to the Sahara Desert. The rulers of **Mali** established the Muslim religion that had come out of Arabia and was sweeping throughout Africa. Mali's most well-known king, Mansa Musa, advanced his civilization to a point of such great wealth that when he made his pilgrimage to Mecca, he spent more than a *hundred camel-loads of gold* on his holy trip. Perhaps, because of such abuses by its kings, **Mali**, once one of the world's great trading nations, was eventually conquered by the neighboring kingdom of **Songhai (Songhay)**.

- **Songhai (Songhay)**   The Sunni dynasty of **Songhai** conquered **Mali** after **Mali** had progressively grown weaker with its line of ineffective kings. By the 1470s, **Songhai** had become the largest and richest country in Africa, boasting the city of Timbuktu, which was the center of learning and trade for the Muslim world. In Timbuktu, men and boys (only) studied at its great university, utilizing to great advantage its many active libraries and books on history, medicine, astronomy and poetry. The first **Songhai** king, Sunni Ali, destroyed much of Timbuktu, but his successor, Askia, rebuilt this ancient city of learning. However, after the death of Askia, the **Songhai Empire** weakened and was finally conquered by neighboring enemies. Timbuktu, once the center of learning, became a tiny desert town, important only because of its history.

  After the fall of the **Songhai Empire**, the days of the great black kingdoms of West Africa were over.

  Attesting to Hansberry's preoccupation with the demise of such great African civilizations and her deep regret that there was a universal lack of knowledge of these ancient black kingdoms are her constant references to Africa in *Raisin*. **Ghana, Mali,** and **Songhai** were the three greatest of the many empires that flourished in West Africa; yet all that remains of these advanced civilizations of past great wealth and strength are relics of ruins and the tales of ancient travelers.

- **Benin**   When George Murchison mentions "the great sculpture of Benin," he is referring to the magnificent works of art that were produced throughout Africa, much to the astonished appreciation of Europeans who had come to Africa, first to trade and later to capture slaves. But, of all the superior works of art that came out of Africa, the most remarkable were those found in Benin.

Many factors contributed to the downfall of the aforementioned empires, including weakening from within by internal strife, invasions by outsiders and the beginnings of trade along the West Coast with European merchants.

The coastal people who had once been ruled by empires in the interior soon began to trade slaves and gold for firearms and ammunition, since lances, spears, and arrows were no match against the rifles and cannons of the Arabs and Europeans. Using their new weapons to fight their rulers, they eventually created their own kingdoms in the coastal forests of West Africa, the most powerful of which was that of Benin (present-day Nigeria).

Benin's theocracy dictated the production of art for religious purposes. Tradition states that around 1170, the Oba (king) commissioned the finest bronze/brass-smith, a man who was so excellent in his craft that to this day, his name is worshipped as a god by the bronze/brass-smiths of Benin. Thus began the Benin practice of making bronze-brass castings to memorialize important events.

Sadly, the people of Benin began to involve themselves in the lucrative Atlantic slave-trade — selling captured rival prisoners to Europeans and Americans.

At this point, we should note that although Hansberry lauds the Ashanti empires specifically and speaks highly of the art of Benin through the dialogue of her character, Beneatha, Hansberry, herself, in other essays, refers specifically to the Ashanti as "those murderous, slave trading Ashanti." Hansberry does *not* mention the slave trading aspect of West African history in this play; possibly she believed that this fact would be intentionally misinterpreted. The inexcusable complicity of the Africans in the heinous slave trade, however miniscule it might have been, is often exaggerated — perhaps, in an attempt to assuage guilt over the grand scale involvement in the violation of human rights by all those connected with the Atlantic slave trade.

As the economy of Benin grew to depend upon the slave trade, internal strife once again claimed an empire as Benin declined and was eventually overwhelmed by the British. The British attack on Benin, ironically, was initially to retaliate for the killing of nine European travelers. But when the British stormed the city, they were so impressed by the Benin bronzes that they took them back with them, giving the British Museum an incomparable collection of rare treasures of African art. Because this art received such worldwide attention, few wanted to believe that such magnificent artwork had been created by the Africans. Thus, the art of Benin was, at first, attributed to the Portuguese; then someone suggested that the bronzes had been washed ashore from the lost city of Atlantis or had been created by its descendants or survivors; others said that some lost and wandering Europeans had found themselves in Benin and had produced the bronze wonders; others said that nomadic Greeks had produced these works while journeying through Africa. Still others insisted that these works, found in Africa, had been the products of the European Renaissance. All of this confusion was due to the widespread ignorance of Africa, its traditions, its people and their capabilities, and the great lost civilizations. In this play Hansberry attempted, in her own small way, to educate the world about Africa through her drama about a poor black family living on Chicago's Southside.

- **Bantu**   The Bantu language is the tongue common to the peoples of Africa who live below the equator. There are many languages and tribes among the Bantu people —thus, the Bantu are one of the many native African groups who speak one of the Bantu languages. Bantu is the largest language family and Swahili (which consists of Bantu and Arabic) is the most widely spoken.

- **that big hotel on the Drive**   Walter refers to "that big hotel on the Drive" in a conversation with George Murchison as he asks George about the Murchison family's prospective real estate ventures. Clearly, Hansberry uses her own family's livelihood as being the livelihood of the rich black family in *Raisin*. Lorraine Hansberry's father was a successful real estate businessman; apparently, the Murchison family of *Raisin* is equally successful for Walter refers to the Murchisons' purchase of a big hotel on the "Drive." The "Drive" to which Walter refers is an expressway along a scenic stretch of land —a large sprawling park or a river view; in whatever city, this would be expensive property. In 1959, any one, most especially a black person, who could afford to purchase a hotel —especially a hotel on such expensive property —would have been very wealthy.

- **Prometheus**   As noted later in the character analysis of Walter Lee Younger, George Murchison's reference to Prometheus fits Walter's fiery personality, along with several other parallels. Prometheus, the god who was punished for having brought fire to mortals, was chained to Mt. Caucasus, where his liver was torn out every day by an eagle but grew back each night. Prometheus' suffering lasted for thousands of years — until Hercules killed the eagle and freed Prometheus. Although Walter's frustrations of establishing his own business appear to devour his hopes, his obsession with his dream restores his hope. George is pedantic, showing off his knowledge, when he says to Walter (after he is safely half-out the door), "Good night, Prometheus."

- **Gimme some sugar then**   A southern expression that means "Give me a hug, a kiss." Mama says this to Travis as she tells him about the house that she is planning to buy.

• **never been 'fraid of no crackers**   After Mama has announced her plans to buy a house in an all-white neighborhood, Ruth at first expresses fear. Then, as if it were an afterthought, Ruth says that she's "never been 'fraid of no crackers" even though her previous dialogue says otherwise. Traditionally, "crackers" refers to bigoted whites, especially those living in Georgia; here, Ruth is using the term to derogatorily refer to all white racists.

ACT II—SCENE 2

Summary

The scene opens a few weeks later, on a Friday night; packing crates fill the Younger apartment in preparation for the move. Beneatha and George come in from their date and after a brief disagreement, George leaves, puzzled. Mama, still smarting over Walter's previous accusation that she "butchered" his dream, decides to entrust Walter with the responsibility for the remaining money, stipulating that he first deposit $3,000 for Beneatha's education. Filled with renewed hope, Walter tells Travis about his dreams for the future and says that he is about to embark on a new venture—a transaction that will change their lives.

In this scene, another character is introduced, a neighbor, Mrs. Johnson. This character, however, was cut from the original stage production in order to reduce production costs. The most recent editions (the complete version) of *Raisin* includes this character, as did the American Playhouse presentation of this play.

When Mrs. Johnson enters, she brings the Youngers a newspaper that tells of a bombing of a black family's home in an all-white neighborhood. Mrs. Johnson's intent is clearly to belittle the importance of the Youngers' getting away from the horrid conditions of their cramped apartment. Still, her warning to the Youngers was a reality in 1959, when this play opened, and, unfortunately, in some communities, even today.

Commentary

Hansberry makes it clear here that George and Beneatha are not compatible. Because of their strong philosophical differences, any marriage between these two is destined to fail. George tells Beneatha that she is too much of an intellectual and that men don't like opinionated, liberated women. He also says that Beneatha is a bit too "moody" and artistic; he tells her that he didn't ask her to go on a date with him to discuss her "thoughts."

Beneatha uses George's weak attempts to change her personality as the excuse that she needs to end their relationship. Later, Beneatha is surprised that Mama agrees with her decision about George, which indicates a softening of the tensions that had previously plagued their relationship.

The "Mrs. Johnson" character brings laughter to the scene, for she is a comical figure, but she also expresses sentiments that have always been prevalent in the black community. She compares, for example, the overt racism of the south at that time with the covert racism found in the north. In 1959, when this play opened, many blacks who had only recently left the south were surprised to find a different type of racism in the north. Mrs. Johnson's implication is that it is easier to survive the blatant racism of a 1959 southern town than it is to be prepared for the hidden, and therefore more dangerous, racism of the urban ghettos.

After Mrs. Johnson leaves and Mama learns that Walter has not been to work in three days, she feels responsible for his despair ("I been doing to you what the rest of the world been doing to you"), so responsible, in fact, that she gives him $6500, all that's left of the insurance check after her downpayment of $3500 on the Clybourne Park house, so that he can feel that he is the "man of the house." She stipulates that $3000 is to go in a savings account for Beneatha's medical schooling, but it is not clear that he even hears Mama. He is overwhelmed and his sudden exuberance over this financial windfall leads him to share some of his many fantasies with Travis.

Walter's already exaggerated dreams, however, suddenly turn into an avalanche of pitiful prattle. He says, for example, that one day he will come in from work, ". . . home from my office downtown . . . ," and even Travis is incredulous as he reminds his father, "You don't work in no office, Daddy." Walter can not seem to stop, though, and the more he talks to Travis about his dream, the bigger the dream gets. The bigger the dream gets, the more preposterous it sounds because Walter soon begins to talk about his future gardener, to whom he has given the first name of "Jefferson"! It is then that we realize that Walter has reached a "point of no return." He must either take action now to make his dream a reality or just give up on his dream altogether.

- **Drop the Garbo routine** When George Murchison admonishes Beneatha to "drop the Garbo routine," he is telling her to know her "place" as a woman. Beneatha intellectualizes everything, is clearly independent, does not defer to men, and argues whatever points of chauvinism she finds in her conversation with men. George wants Beneatha to be more quiet and submissive. He implies in his speech that men do not like aggressive, independent, liberated women and that if she ever hopes to get married and have a family, she is going to have to "drop the Garbo routine," meaning she will have to stop studying and thinking so much, and start acting "like a [submissive] woman."

- **the nature of quiet desperation** The complete quotation to which George refers is "The mass of men lead lives of quiet desperation," a line from Thoreau's *Walden*. George proves to be as pedantic as Beneatha, peppering his arguments with literary allusions and oftentimes esoteric references—for example, calling Walter "Prometheus." George is trying to persuade Beneatha to abandon her feminist principles when he utters this philosophical truth, but throughout the play, Hansberry shows that many of the characters in *Raisin* do indeed lead lives of quiet desperation: Mama, although outwardly strong, is consumed with anxiety over the various, disparate directions her children are going; Walter Lee is clearly a desperate man, trying to secure a dream that eludes him; Ruth is pregnant but afraid to have this child (one more mouth to feed), especially since it will be born into a marital relationship that is deteriorating from within; Beneatha is desperately seeking her own identity while simultaneously attempting to escape the stereotypical barriers of her class and gender; and last, even Karl Lindner is a desperate man, rationalizing his rigid beliefs in a rapidly changing world.

  Of all the characters, Asagai appears to be the most serene; even when his is contemplating justifiable reasons for anxiety—that is, the political turmoil within his homeland and the possibility of his own death in his desire for his country's independence. Note that Asagai calmly accepts whatever his fate might be and even becomes an inadvertent peacemaker when he diffuses Beneatha's vitriolic reaction to Walter's loss of the family's money.

- **He's got a conked head** A "conked head" refers to a hairstyle adopted by some black men during the forties and early fifties. Because of what was defined as "self hatred" by psychologists who studied the phenomenon, oftentimes a group that believes itself to be oppressed will mimic the life-style and, sometimes, even mimic the appearance of the "dominant group." During this period in history, some black men (especially those connected with show business) would have their hair straightened through a chemi-cal process that was both demeaning and extremely painful. Looking at old photographs of Nat King Cole, Sam Cooke, Little Richard, Chuck Berry and other entertainers of that period, we see that they adopted this style. Many times though, men within the criminal element in the black com-munity also wore their hair in this "conked" style when the style became a symbol of affluence. As a result, people within the black community often had negative perceptions about those who adopted this style. If those men were not a part of the entertainment industry, they were either denizens of the underworld or full-fledged or potential gangsters.

The person whom Walter Lee describes as having a "conked head" is a part of the entertainment world; he is a musician at the Green Hat, a bar that Walter Lee frequents.

- **the best little combo in the world**   This phrase refers to the band of musicians that Walter admires in the Green Hat. "Combo" is a synonym for "band." Clearly, we can see by the way Walter talks about them that he appreciates their music very much.

- **peckerwoods**   no-count riff-raff; poor, shiftless, racially prejudiced whites.

- **Booker T. Washington**   Booker T. Washington (1856–1915) was one of the most influential black leaders during the period immediately follow-ing Reconstruction (1865–77). Extremely hard working, he attended school at night. When he heard about Hampton Institute in Virginia, a school for blacks, he enrolled in order to study brick masonry, paying for his educa-tion by working as the janitor. Known mainly for his founding of Tuskegee Institute, Washington believed that blacks should be educated only by trade schools. He felt that they should develop manual skills and improve their craft at the building trades and that blacks should become experts in farm-ing. (One of Washington's first staff appointments was Dr. George Wash-ington Carver, whose brilliance in the field of agriculture is not as well documented as his "peanut" discoveries.) Washington believed strongly that artistic endeavors and intellectual pursuits were not in the best inter-est of black people trying to emerge from a long period of slavery. Wash-ington felt that having a trade was more logical for black people than painting or poetry.

In his "Atlanta speech," Booker T. Washington urged blacks to cultivate friendly relations with white men. He suggested that blacks devote them-selves to agriculture, mechanics, domestic service, and the professions —

placing more value on acquiring an industrial skill than on attaining a seat in Congress.

Black writers tend to side with **W. E. B. Du Bois,** who believed in the importance of artistic endeavors (which Washington believed to be a frivolous activity). Hansberry has one of her characters call Booker T. Washington a "fool," which is an elitist comment since only the very well read of her audience would even have known of the political rivalry between the two men.

Washington's long-time opponent, W. E. B. Du Bois (1868–1963), was a man who dramatically espoused the opposite of Washington's philosophy. Du Bois, educated at Fisk, Harvard, and the University of Berlin, was a writer and political activist, activities which Washington perceived as frivolous.

Blacks began to "choose sides," debating constantly over who was right, and over which philosophy was actually in the best interest of black people.

Hansberry has the comical character of Mrs. Johnson act as the defender of Booker T. Washington's philosophy, as she says, "I always thinks like Booker T. Washington said that time — 'Education has spoiled many a good plow hand.' " Hansberry, herself, speaks through Mama, who dismisses Washington as a "fool." And when Mrs. Johnson goes on to say that Washington "was one of our great men," Mama counters, almost angrily, with, "Who said so?" The debate does not continue and, at this point, Mrs. Johnson concedes by saying, "You know, me and you ain't never agreed about some things, Lena Younger. I guess I better be going —."

ACT II — SCENE 3

Summary

This scene begins one week later. Ruth and Beneatha are in good spirits; this is the day that the family will move to their new neighborhood. Ruth tells Beneatha that on the previous evening, she and Walter had gone on a date to the movies. Walter comes in and is dancing playfully with Ruth when a white man comes to the door, asking for Lena Younger. Walter tries on his new status as "head of the household," telling the stranger that he handles his mother's "business matters."

The man, Karl Lindner, acting as representative of the Clybourne Park Improvement Association, makes a very generous offer to buy the Youngers' new home (in order to keep them from moving into Clybourne Park). At first, Walter listens then tells Lindner to get out. When Lena returns, they each try to shield her from the reality that

Lindner represents by giving her the housewarming gifts they'd purchased. Soon afterwards, Bobo arrives to tell Walter that Willy ran off with their money. Both Mama and Walter explode with feelings of loss, anger, helplessness, and grief.

Commentary

When the curtain rises, Ruth is singing a well-known spiritual, "No Ways Tired," the same song that Mama asked Ruth to sing at the close of Act I, Scene 1, just before she realized that Ruth had fainted. At the end of Act I, Scene 1, Ruth is overwhelmed with fatigue, compounded by an unplanned pregnancy. These facts give the lie to the title of the song and end the act with dark irony.

When Act II, Scene 3 opens, Ruth is singing this song without waiting for someone to ask her. The significance of the song lies in its words: **I don't feel no ways tired. I've come too far from where I started from ... I don't believe He brought me this far — to leave me ...**" The song is proof that there has been a resurgence of faith among the members of the Younger household. Mama, however, it is important to note, never relinquishes her faith — not even after she learns that Walter has lost their money; rather than succumb to feelings of despair, Mama cries out to God for strength in dealing with her new crisis.

The song also foreshadows the Youngers' decision to occupy their new home in a new neighborhood — in spite of their fears of what might await them. Interestingly, the song eventually became one of the songs sung by civil rights demonstrators in the early sixties, perhaps because of the popularity of Hansberry's play.

Here in this scene, Hansberry highlights Lindner's weakness in negotiating with the Youngers. He is not straightforward or honest, so considerable time is wasted before they actually know what he is actually proposing. Beneatha, however, distrusts Lindner immediately; the "thirty pieces of silver" to which she alludes refers to the betrayal of Christ for that paltry sum. But neither Walter nor Ruth trusts Beneatha's quick judgment of a white person because of Beneatha's almost obsessive pro-African stance. Walter even tells Beneatha to be quiet and "let the man talk" when Beneatha tries to interrupt Lindner.

After Lindner is ordered out of the apartment and Mama returns, they give her the housewarming gifts. Now that Mama's dream of having a garden is about to become a reality, gardening tools are appropriate, as is Travis' special present of a gardening hat. Travis intended his present to be a symbol of Lena's new "rich woman's" status, for he has seen wealthy women in magazines wearing similar hats. Ironically, though, Travis' gift serves more to make Mama look like a field hand than a wealthy woman, ready to go out and inspect her spacious garden.

In this scene Walter too sings a Negro spiritual, anticipating all the money he will make from his secret deal. The song "Heaven" was sung by the slaves in order to ridicule the slave owners in code. The line: "Everybody talkin' 'bout heaven ain't goin' there . . ." was the slaves' way of poking fun at the slave owners who were often "religious" and had no doubts that they would eventually get to heaven. Walter's singing the song has a special meaning to him because he is "on top of the world," anticipating a happy future for himself. However, Bobo's arrival proves that the one key line in the song which Walter *does not* sing will have major significance in Walter's fortunes — that is, for the present at least, Walter is *not* "gonna walk all over God's heaven."

- **hand-turned hems** This refers to sewing that is done "by hand" and not in a factory on a machine. Ruth has purchased some curtains for the new house, proof of her exuberance over the possibility of their moving away from the ghetto, for Ruth did not even measure the windows before rushing out and buying curtains. When she is asked if she considered whether these curtains will even fit the windows of the new house, Ruth says, "Oh well, they bound to fit something . . ." The curtains, she brags, have "hand-turned hems," which would, of course, make them more valuable than machine-made curtains.

- **Thirty pieces and not a coin less** Thirty pieces of silver was the standard price of a slave (Exodus 21:32). Judas Iscariot betrayed Jesus Christ for the same amount of money (30 pieces of silver) normally paid for a slave. Beneatha taunts Lindner with this allusion when he makes his generous offer to keep the Younger family out of the neighborhood.

- **Mrs. Miniver** An Oscar-winning film (1942) which starred Greer Garson as Mrs. Miniver, an English middle-class housewife who appears in many scenes tending her roses. In the movie, despite the blitz bombs of Nazi Germany, Mrs. Miniver stands stalwart, the symbol of England's hope and strength. Because Mama's housewarming gift is a set of gardening tools, the card reads, "To our own Mrs. Miniver . . ." Mama's strength and her survival in a nation divided by racial struggle makes her an appropriate parallel to Mrs. Miniver.

• **Scarlett O'Hara**   When Travis gives Mama his gift, of which he is enormously proud, everyone laughs because it is an oversized gardening hat worn, as he says, by [rich] ladies "who always have it on when they work in their gardens." However, instead of looking like a rich "lady" in her garden, in this hat, Mama looks more like a slave who is about to pick cotton, which makes everyone laugh. Mama doesn't want to hurt Travis' feelings, so she tells him how much she likes it even though she probably knows better than the others how ridiculous she looks in the hat. Beneatha laughs and says that their intention in giving the gardening tools was to make Mama look like Mrs. Miniver, while Travis' gift makes Mama look more like Scarlett O'Hara (from Mitchell's *Gone With the Wind*, a novel that laments the fall of the South after the Civil War).

• **spread some money 'round**   Walter Lee had previously explained to Bobo that the only way to make "big" money was through the payment of required graft, which Walter Lee refers to as having to "spread some money 'round." Bobo is apparently too intellectually dense to understand that this is a term that one does not use openly. Bobo uses the expression casually, as though it were conversationally correct.

ACT III

Summary

An hour later, having no knowledge of the Youngers' financial reversals, Asagai drops by the apartment, hoping to help with the packing, but instead he is greeted by a changed Beneatha. Seemingly, she is in shock. Very simply, she states, "He gave away the money . . ." Her previous positive idealism has been replaced by a loss of faith in humanity. The money that should have financed her medical education is gone.

She wants and expects sympathy from Asagai, but instead, he upbraids her for her materialistic outlook. (Later, in her often quoted ". . . measure him right" speech, Mama too will challenge Beneatha's egocentric perceptions concerning the loss of the money.) Beneatha listens, then agrees to consider Asagai's proposal of marriage, along with his invitation that she move to Nigeria to practice medicine.

Later, Walter comes in and begins searching frantically for Lindner's telephone number, while ignoring Beneatha's insults. Mama suggests that they give up on their dream of moving and that they make themselves satisfied with the apartment in which they are presently living, a suggestion that seems to upset Ruth more than anyone else.

Shortly thereafter, we learn that Walter has decided to accept Lindner's offer of paying them generously not to move in. Aghast, the three Younger women watch Walter rehearse an exaggerated servility with which he plans to greet Lindner. However, moved by Mama's word about black pride, Walter changes his mind and disappoints Lindner. He tells him that he and his family have decided to live in Clybourne Park.

Commentary

Through Asagai, we see that the African struggle for independence is similar to Walter's struggle for independence; however, at the same time, Hansberry expresses her own fears that the new black leadership of the emerging African nations might prove to be as corruptly oppressive as the previous colonial rulers. Ironically, Walter achieves his independence —that is, he comes "into his manhood" *without* the money that has been his obsession throughout the play. Previously, Walter stated that his self worth was predicated on the amount of money he could garner or generate. He is broke now and feeling foolish over his egregious error, but he has a more realistic and mature vision of what independence means and demands of individuals. It is also through Asagai that we are made aware of the Western definition of success, as he questions the happiness one should expect through money gained because of someone's death.

Hansberry also uses the final scene to show us the maturation of each character, including Mama, who has learned while teaching. When she tells Beneatha that the true test of love is the ability to love a person when he is at his lowest, we realize that Mama has had time to reflect upon this fact herself.

- **Monsieur le petit bourgeois noir**   Beneatha is so angry at Walter Lee for having entrusted their family's money to the unscrupulous Willy that she mockingly derides Walter Lee for having shown such mercantile naivete. To Beneatha, it is apparent that Walter Lee's financial folly was due to his total lack of knowledge about the workings of the business world; she taunts him by referring to him as "Monsieur le petit bourgeois noir," meaning "Mister [black] small businessman." She goes on to taunt him by calling him other names, such as "Symbol of the Rising Class," "Entrepreneur," "Titan of the System," and "Chairman of the Board," none of which Walter is and few of which Walter has ever heard. By calling Walter Lee "Monsieur le petit bourgeois noir," Beneatha gives us proof that she is oppressively pedantic since she is clearly showing off her learning and is bragging (once again) about her college student status. She speaks mostly for her own emotional benefit, for she knows that Walter has no knowledge of the meaning of her words in French, just as he barely understands the meaning of the insults she hurls at him in English.

- **peachy keen, as the ofay kids say**   This is a reference to the racial differences in language, most especially in the area of slang. When *Raisin* opened in 1959, the expression "peachy keen" was common to white teenagers, as was "swell," both of which were used to refer to something that was "good," while in the black communities, "boss," "zanzy," or "bad" were used to refer to something "good." In addition, the word "ofay" was a slang word used in the black communities at that time to refer to a white person. (It is the word "foe" in the nonsense language of Pig Latin, in which the first letter of a word is placed at the end with the addition of the long "A" sound. "Pig" would become "Igpay"; in order to refer to a white person as a "foe," one would say "ofay.")

    This is somewhat of a testament to the racial climate of the country in 1959, when fears of reprisals often had blacks concealing their negative feelings in the code words of slang.

    Translated then, "Peachy keen, as the ofay kids say" means "That's very good — as the white kids would say."

- **Lena Eggleston is a high-minded thing**   Mama is so distraught over Walter's having lost the family's remaining money that, at first, she decides against moving into Clybourne Park and tries to make herself satisfied with the thought of remaining in her cramped Southside apartment. Mama reminisces about her youth and how she had always wanted more than what had been offered to her. She realizes now, she says, in her moment of defeat, that she was foolish to set her sights so high. She says that everyone around her used to laugh at her; they would say, "That Lena Eggleston is a high-minded thing. She'll get her due one day." Mama implies that perhaps her misfortune now is the "due" that her detractors warned her of.

- **sharecroppers**   Many blacks were sharecroppers in the south before the mass exodus of blacks to the northern cities. A sharecropper lives on someone else's farmland and pays, as his rent, a large share of the crop he yields from this farmland. Sharecroppers were, for this reason, poor; it was nearly

tells the story of Walter Lee —granted that his is a story greatly influenced by Mama. A proud woman, Lena Younger does not have much material wealth, but she walks tall, exudes dignity, and carries herself, as Hansberry says, with the "noble bearing of the women of the Heroes of Southwest Africa [a pastoral people] ...," as though she walks with a "basket or a vessel upon her head." Her children are her life; she refers to them as her "harvest." With no significant dreams of her own, she lives vicariously through her children, for even her dream of having a house is motivated only by her desire to make living conditions better for her family. She says, upon receiving the $10,000 insurance check that, for her part, she'd just as soon donate the entire sum to her church.

Because Mama seems to be accustomed to suffering and enduring hardships, the Lindners of the world cannot disturb her inner peace, for she has previously suffered the death of a baby and, more recently, the death of her husband of many years. Her strong faith and deep religious convictions give her the psychological and physical mettle she needs in order to rise to life's challenges. At her lowest point, she asks God to replenish her waning strength and is immediately possessed of a more compassionate perception of Walter Lee's folly.

Mama's old-fashioned and conservative views are evident when she speaks of her husband's past "womanizing" and chauvinistic behavior as being something that she could overlook. Mama actually believes that accepting such behavior is a woman's lot in life. Ruth, however, is only slightly more liberated as she, too, would accept such behavior in her man, but she would at least address the problem. Beneatha, in contrast, represents a new, liberated generation of women; she would never accept such behavior in a man and would, perhaps, have spoken out against Mama's lack of spunk in dealing with a sexist mate had Mama reminisced about life with "Big Walter" with Beneatha instead of Ruth.

Mama's single weakness appears to be her all-consuming love for her grandson, Travis, which causes her to spoil him and causes her also to act in a somewhat meddlesome manner with her daughter-in-law. Mama impresses us with her strength, but this strength appears to have been sublimated during her marriage. It seems that only after the death of "Big Walter," when Mama has to become head of the household, that she can summon the herculean strength she exhibits throughout the drama.

As her name suggests, Lena's entire family "leans on" her and draws from her strength in order to replenish their own.

WALTER LEE YOUNGER ("BROTHER")

Essentially, this play is the story of Walter Lee Younger, sometimes called "Brother." Passionate, ambitious and bursting with the energy of his dreams, Walter Lee is a desperate man, shackled by poverty and prejudice, and obsessed with a business idea that he thinks will solve all of his economic and social problems. He believes, for example, that through his business idea, he will suddenly accumulate all the money he will ever need. Then, with this sudden accumulation of capital, he will improve himself socially and will be looked up to by others —all the people who, he believes, do not think much of him as a man.

He will, he believes, finally be able to provide material necessities and even luxuries for his wife. Walter asks in desperation why shouldn't *his* wife wear pearls. Who decides, he wonders, which women *should* wear pearls in this world. However, Walter proves throughout the drama that he does not possess the entrepreneurial skills necessary to succeed in business. His education is sorely lacking, a fact made most clear in his confrontation with George Murchison. When George says, "Good night Prometheus," Walter not only does not know what "Prometheus" refers to, but he actually thinks that George, just that moment, made up the word.

The word "Prometheus" fits Walter's fiery personality. Prometheus, the god who was punished for bringing fire to mortals, was chained to Mt. Caucasus, where every day an eagle tore out his liver, which grew back each night. Prometheus' suffering lasted for thousands of years —until Hercules killed the eagle and freed Prometheus. As a parallel, Walter, too, is chained, and likewise, his obsessive dream restores what his frustrations devour. Sadly, Walter never sees any way out of his economic distress other than the liquor store, which his mother opposes solely on moral grounds. Nowhere in the play does Mama indicate that she would not give Walter the money for some *other* business idea; it's just that she resists the idea of his selling liquor. Walter's singular obsession causes him to lose sight of his possible alternatives and of a compromise that might have led to his goal of economic independence. Walter's chauvinism is evident immediately when he tells his wife, Ruth, that for a fleeting moment, she "looked young ... real young ... but ... it's gone now ..." Walter Lee is older than Ruth, but, to him, looking young is important only to a woman. However, it is, perhaps, the disturbing realization of his *own* aging that prompts his sarcasm, for shortly after these remarks to both, he admits that he has been contemplating his own aging, without having realized any of his dreams, when he says, "This morning, I was lookin' in the mirror and thinking about it ... I'm thirty-five years old; I been married eleven years and I got a boy who sleeps in the living room ..."

Walter's chauvinism is further apparent when he questions Beneatha about her decision to become a doctor: he asks why she couldn't just become a nurse or get married "like other women." When he comes home after a drinking bout with his friends and Beneatha is dancing to the African music, he says, "Shut up" to Ruth, just before joining Beneatha in the dance. Walter is obsessed with getting money so that he can buy "things for Ruth"; he is unaware that treating Ruth more kindly and with more respect would be more appreciated and valued than any "gifts."

After Walter foolishly entrusts all of his mother's remaining money to his unscrupulous buddy, his shame turns to self hatred, the only emotion that permits him to consider selling out his race and accepting Lindner's offer. It is a proud moment when Walter, mainly because Travis is watching him, cannot bring himself to relinquish his remaining dignity for Lindner's offer of money.

BENEATHA YOUNGER

Because Beneatha is the most educated of the Youngers, she sometimes seems to be obnoxious and self-centered; especially in the early scenes, she freely verbalizes her views in a household that has difficulty understanding her perspectives. She favors her African suitor over her rich boyfriend, much to the puzzlement of her family.

Even though her family is clearly poor, Beneatha has no reservations about feeding her ego. We learn that she "flits" from one expensive hobby to another as her mood dictates, even though it often seems that the family could use the money spent on Beneatha's horseback riding, her camera equipment, her acting lessons, and her guitar lessons for other, more financially relevant things.

Beneatha's "schooling" is a privilege that Walter Lee has not had, yet Beneatha appears to believe that a higher education is her right.

Everyone in the family is making a sacrifice so that Beneatha can become a doctor —a fact pointed out by Walter Lee as they clash in the first scene of the play. Yet beneath what seems to be selfishness, Beneatha's strengths are her spirit of independence, the fact that she is a "new woman" who refuses to accept the traditional, spineless female role, and the fact that she is so knowledgeable about Africa that her self-esteem is enhanced. Beneatha's search for her identity is a motif carried throughout the play; the closer she gets to Africa via her relationship with Joseph Asagai, the more she develops into a pleasant, likeable, and less egocentric person.

Beneatha's relationship with her mother is largely one of conflict because of their many differences, but it is not a strained relationship, for even after her mother slaps her for her blasphemous talk, Beneatha later hugs and thanks her mother for understanding her dismissal of George. She clearly loves her mother even if they do not always agree. Beneatha *is* opinionated, especially in her dealings with her brother, Walter Lee; she clearly lives up to her name, an obvious pun, for, especially at the beginning of the play, everything and everyone seem to be "beneath her."

JOSEPH ASAGAI

An African student, Joseph Asagai courts the attentions of Beneatha. In trying to win her affections, he is persistent but never overbearing. He flatters her with gifts (something that George Murchison has not done); in addition, Asagai's gifts are not meaningless trinkets but are things that are both useful to and desired by Beneatha —such as the Nigerian robes he clearly has gone to a lot of trouble to obtain. Asagai's compliments to Beneatha are sincere and therefore believable. His peaceful ways and calm manner give Beneatha an appreciation of his views even when they disagree. Contrasted with George Murchison's abrasive put-downs of Beneatha and George's insistence on retaining his narrow-minded views, Asagai appears as Beneatha's savior from the potential tragedy of her eventually becoming George's wife.

Asagai is charming, mannerly, personable and quite intelligent; in spite of the cultural differences between him and the Younger family, he appears to "fit in" more with them than does George Murchison, who argues with Beneatha in front of her family and then clashes with Walter as he leaves.

45

Asagai is zealously idealistic about the future of his country and has even expressed his willingness to sacrifice his own life for the independence of his country. And, although Asagai has been afforded a Western education, his basic beliefs are grounded in his own African culture, which was, as of 1959, somewhat chauvinistic and old-fashioned. This creates an undercurrent of tension in his relationship with Beneatha, but it is something that Hansberry hints that might be overcome.

Asagai is helpful and concerned about the welfare of others. He volunteers to assist in the move to Clybourne Park and offers much-needed consolation and good advice to Beneatha when she is at her lowest. He counsels Beneatha spiritually and emotionally, helping her to get back "on track" as she rails against her brother's foolishness in having lost the money.

Asagai's philosophy runs counter to the Western perception of success at any cost. He questions, for example, the satisfaction of receiving money through misfortune while calling it "success." He contrasts this view with his own that "making it" via insurance money gained through misfortune is not really "making it." Asagai's character gives Beneatha political focus and nourishes her idealism. Being a true African, Asagai is grounded in his "Africaness" while Beneatha is trying, almost too hard, to connect with an African past that she knows so little of. It is Beneatha and not Asagai who is constantly singing the praises of Africa.

The name of Hansberry's African character is taken from the word "assegai," which means a short-handled stabbling spear, famous in the successful ware of Shaka Zulu.

GEORGE MURCHISON

In this play, the educated and wealthy George Murchison represents the black person whose own self-hatred manifests itself as contempt for other blacks. George is pedantic—an academic show-off—constantly making literary allusions even when he knows that this information is lost upon his audience. When Ruth asks George what time the play begins that he's taking Beneatha to see, he answers pompously, "It's an eight-thirty curtain. That's just Chicago, though. In New York, standard curtain time is eight-forty." Such information is wasted on Ruth, who has probably never seen a play and certainly has never been to New York. Note here that Ruth asks, "What time is the show?" as if it is a movie or entertainment other than the legitimate theater.

George's pomposity won't even permit him to ignore Walter's desperate lie that he knows what New York is like; "Oh, you've been?" George asks in order to further belittle a man whose self-esteem is already zero. When Beneatha mentions Africa, George begins immediately to recite everything he knows about African civilizations. Even though he clearly has no respect for any of the accomplishments of the Negro people, still George is compelled to match his knowledge against Beneatha's.

When George and Beneatha argue just before their inevitable breakup, he warns Beneatha not to be such a serious intellectual and free-thinking "new woman." But, when he says, "I don't go out with you to discuss the nature of 'quiet desperation,'" he is showing off his own accumulation of learning. The phrase "quiet desperation" comes from a line in Henry David Thoreau's *Walden:* "Most men lead lives of quiet desperation."

KARL LINDNER

The Lindner character, although basically a "flat character," is still developed by Hansberry as a human being and not simply a stereotype of a bigot. For example, when Mr. Lindner arrives at the Younger household, he is extremely shy and timid, not threatening or abrasive or loud. He is polite, and mannerly, even though everything he says is insulting to the Youngers.

It is immediately apparent to us that Mr. Lindner is not even aware of his insults to them. He is simply a courier from the Clybourne Park neighborhood, bringing a message to the Youngers that he, himself, had no part in originating. He has been sent by the organization which he represents, and he naively believes in the correctness of this organization. But, never do we get the impression that Lindner is filled with hatred that would make him knowingly insult the Youngers or hurt them physically in any way. Lindner does not realize the scope of his mission. When he says that "people want to live among their own kind, . . ." he firmly believes that he is doing the Youngers a favor by offering to pay them *not* to move into Clybourne Park.

The Youngers are kind to Lindner when he first enters their apartment, and Lindner's amazement turns into discomfort. When they offer Lindner refreshments, he declines because he realizes at this point that the Youngers are decent people, which makes his mission uncomfortable for him. Lindner appears almost pathetic as he tries to explain his point of view to a fiery Beneatha, an angry Walter, and a surprised Ruth.

MRS. JOHNSON (MRS. WILHELMINA OTHELLA JOHNSON)

The character of Mrs. Johnson appears mostly for comic relief. She is a flat caricature of the nosy, jealous neighbor. However, Hansberry employs the Mrs. Johnson character in order to point out the explosive realities that await the Youngers for being the first blacks to move into Clybourne Park. Mrs. Johnson is insensitive and unkind, asking indelicate, overly nosy questions. At one point, she practically says outright that she is hoping that the Youngers' new house will be bombed. Although her warnings are about a very real danger to the Youngers, Mrs. Johnson's manner is so offensive that she appears almost ludicrous.

BOBO

Bobo is, as his name suggests, somewhat dimwitted, but he is basically honest and appears to be a loyal friend. When he comes to Walter's apartment to deliver the bad news about the insurance money, he is so mannerly and polite to the women in the Younger household that he appears almost ridiculous. As soon as we meet Bobo, we know instantly why Walter's business idea did not work out as he hoped it would.

Bobo looks to Walter for direction, for even as unschooled as Walter might have appeared to us initially, we see that Walter is far brighter than Bobo. Bobo's thought processes are sluggish; we see that he hardly knows the right words to use as he tries to explain to Walter what happened to their money. We know that Bobo is not bright when he says, "... Me and Willy was going to go down to Springfield and spread some money 'round so's we wouldn't have to wait so long for the liquor license ... everybody said that was the way you had to do ..." We pity Bobo because of his shabby appearance, his limited intelligence, and his inability to ever escape his environment. We, the audience, are more aware of his suffering than Bobo, who is, throughout a pathetic intellectual dwarf.

THE TWO MOVING MEN

Although the moving men have no speaking parts, their few moments on stage are memorable. They are admonished by Mama for not handling her furniture with the care she feels her furniture deserves. The moving men remind us of Walter; maybe their dreams are as intense as Walter's. As they look around the apartment, it appears that they are impressed by the Youngers' dramatic move out of the Southside neighborhood.

WILLY

Although we never meet Willy, we know a lot about him, based upon things that are said about him by the other characters. Willy has no loyalty toward Walter or Bobo: he absconded with their money. Although he knows that he is robbing two people who have as little as he has, this does not stop him; he takes their money and runs off, anyway. Willy is the smartest of the three because he has no illusions about getting rich through Walter's liquor store idea. Willy feels that the most realistic method of his ever escaping poverty is to take the money that Walter and Bobo are foolish enough to entrust to him. Willy would never have entrusted his life savings with either of them. Willy has learned, as Walter says in his speech about the "takers" and the "tooken," how to survive on the streets. He is not bound by moral codes or religious convictions and, therefore, feels no compunction about taking advantage of anyone —not even his close friends.

BIG WALTER

Big Walter is another character whom we never meet and only learn about through the dialogue of others. When Mama reminisces about her life with Big Walter, she speaks of him with admiration, although the audience might question Mama's tolerance of some of his past behavior. Mama says, with a little laugh, that Big Walter was a womanizer, implying that, perhaps, at some point as a young wife, she might have been deeply hurt over Big Walter's antics. We get the impression that he was a very old-fashioned man who dominated his household by his imposing presence. We do learn that Big Walter valued his family over all other priorities. Thus, even if Big Walter did "run around," as Mama laughingly puts it, the implication is that Big Walter would never have left his family —not for any woman.

CRITICAL ESSAYS

APPLYING LITERARY TERMS TO *A RAISIN IN THE SUN*

Didactic literature demonstrates or dramatically presents a thesis or doctrine in a persuasive form. Didactic works attempt to teach a lesson. The term **propaganda** is a sub-division of didactic literature; a work of propaganda undertakes to move the reader to take a position or to take action on a particular moral or political issue of the moment.

Hansberry expresses many political and sociological views in *Raisin,* ideas which attack racism and prejudice; the audience is moved to either take action after having seen the drama or to change previously held bigoted beliefs.

The chief character in a work is called the **protagonist,** or sometimes, the **hero.** Walter is the protagonist in *Raisin,* for even though he does not appear to be a hero in the traditional sense of the word, he is the person around whom the drama revolves. The drama that unfolds in *Raisin* changes Walter dramatically, which prompts Mama to say about him at the end, "He finally come into his manhood today, didn't he? Kind of like a rainbow after the rain . . .''

The most important opponent of the protagonist is called the **antagonist.** In *Raisin,* one might erroneously assume that the antagonist is Karl Lindner, but that is merely a simplistic view. Walter's real opponent is racism. Although Lindner *is* a representative of racist ideas, he is not the only force that is bearing down on Walter, crushing him with its weight.

The relationship between the protagonist and the antagonist is always one of **conflict.** Walter has conflict with Lindner because of what he represents, but Walter's greatest conflict is with all the circumstances that stand between himself and the goal that he is obsessively trying to reach.

Uncertainty about the outcome of the story is known as **suspense.** If what happens in the drama goes against the expectations of the audience, it is known as **surprise.** The relationship between suspense and surprise heightens the magnetic power of the **plot.** In *Raisin,* we are surprised that Mama makes the spontaneous decision to entrust Walter with the remaining $6,500 of the insurance money. Suspense is created by our not knowing exactly what Walter will do with it.

The plot of a drama has **unity of action** if it is complete and orderly, and all of the parts of a plot are necessary to the development of the story. For perfect unity, all of the action must be **significant action**. All events that do not relate to the plot are omitted, which distinguishes literary narrative from merely telling a story of events from real life. All of the events in *Raisin* are necessary to the development of the plot or to the development of the characters. When Walter gives Travis two fifty-cent pieces and then has to return to and get carfare from his wife, we learn a lot about Walter's character: his wanting to shield his son from discovering the family's true economic situation, his feelings of economic inadequacy, and his denial of the ugliness of his family's economic reality.

The German critic Gustav Freytag proposed an analysis of a play as: **rising action, climax,** and **falling action.**

- The **rising action** of the play begins immediately with Walter's obsession with the insurance check that the family is waiting for. He wakes up talking about it, he argues with his sister about it, and he suggests that his wife assist him in his plan to get Mama to sign the check over to him for his business venture. Aristotle used the term **complication** for **rising action.**

- The **climax** of *Raisin* occurs with Bobo's telling Walter that the money is gone and includes the family's immediate response to this tragic news.

- The **falling action** occurs as Walter is contemplating selling his pride for Lindner's money and then deciding not to do so.

The traditional **denouement,** or unravelling of the plot, is the explanation of all the previous events of the drama. After Lindner leaves, we learn through Ruth's dialogue that the family is about to make the move they have spoken of throughout the play —in spite of their sudden financial reversal; Beneatha tells Mama about the marriage proposal that she has received earlier in the day, and Walter and Beneatha's previously troubled familial relationship appears to have been healed.

The **denouement** often includes a **peripety,** sometimes called a reversal, where the hero's fortunes change either for better or worse. In Walter's case, his fortunes change for the better —although initially it may not appear to be so. Walter loses the family's money and is so distraught that he resorts to behavior that indicates self-hatred. Yet, when Walter decides on his own to regain his self-esteem in his dialogue with Lindner, not only does he maintain his own pride, but he also restores the dignity of the entire Younger family.

A **portmanteau word** is the fusion of two meanings packed into one word, as in Lewis Carroll's poem "Jabberwocky," where "slithy" is the combination of "lithe" and "slimy." In *Raisin,* Ruth refers to Travis' "slubborn" ways, when she really means both "sloppy" and "stubborn." Because of Ruth's lack of formal education, she is not aware (but the audience is) that this is not a real word.

One requirement of good literature is that a character's **motivation** — that is, the reasons for his actions — must be consistent with his moral nature and personality. The character may remain the same or the character may go through a complete metamorphosis, but no character should ever break off from the personality we expect of him and suddenly act in a manner that is not a part of his temperament. If the character is real and lifelike, the work is enhanced. Walter's motivation to obtain the insurance money for his business scheme makes all of his subsequent actions believable, even if we feel that they are foolish. Walter's motivation makes all of his dialogue believable and realistic.

A **flat character** is presented only in superficial form, without much individualized detail. A **round character** is more complex and, therefore, more difficult to describe. Mr. Lindner is a flat character, while Walter is a round character; there is no need for the character of Mr. Lindner to be as developed or as detailed as Walter's.

According to Aristotle, the tragic hero will be more dramatically effective if he is an ordinary man, for then the effect of the tragedy will be enhanced as the audience identifies with his pain. **Hamartia** is the "tragic flaw," or "tragic error in judgment," which brings the hero to a momentary defeat. A form of hamartia is the term **hubris,** which means the pride or overconfidence that leads a man to overlook a divine warning or to break a moral law. Walter breaks a moral law when he uses his mother's money for his "get-rich-quick" scheme without telling her; he is not aware of his immorality, for he naively believes that he will get rich and be able to pay her back. In Walter's mind, he is "borrowing" the money that she has entrusted to him. However, Walter knows that his mother has been opposed to his idea of selling liquor because of her religious convictions.

Walter also overlooks a divine warning because both Ruth and Beneatha have, on separate occasions, expressed their feelings about

Willy and Bobo. After Walter has been duped by Willy, Beneatha explains to Asagai that Walter has given away the family's money to a man that ten-year-old "Travis would not have trusted with his most worn out marbles." The tragic hero brings out pity in us because his misfortune is greater than we feel that he deserves, and he brings out fear in us because we recognize similar possibilities and consequences in our own fates.

A **rhetorical question** is asked in order to force the audience or reader to think; one does not expect an answer to a rhetorical question. Should a person exclaim in desperation—"What kind of fool do you think I am?"—this person surely does not expect an answer. In *Raisin*, Walter Lee asks why his wife should not wear pearls. "Who decides," he explodes, "which women should wear pearls in this world?"

Irony is defined as a "twist of fate," which means that the very last thing we would expect to happen, actually does happen. However, irony is not the same as a surprise ending. For example, a much-decorated wartime hero returns to his peaceful suburban village where a parade is planned in his honor. However, just as he is readying himself to join the reviewing stand of his parade, he slips in the shower on a bar of soap, falls, and is immediately and accidentally killed. The irony lies in the fact that he was *not* killed during wartime, which might have been expected. Rather, he was killed in a place where one would have least expected it, *and* the cause of his death has been trivialized as he dies in such a non-heroic manner. In *Raisin*, it is ironic that Walter believes that graft and corruption dominate all successful business activities—even before he is asked to do so, he prepares himself to pay the graft that he thinks will be requested of him—however, when he gives the money to his "friend" (who runs off with it), it is not the unscrupulous collector of graft who robs Walter of his dream; rather, it is his "friend."

Dramatic irony refers to the audience's knowledge of something that the character who is speaking does not know. When the character makes an innocent remark that refers to this "inside knowledge" that the audience has, the character's words contain dramatic irony. For example, as soon as the audience sees Bobo, we are aware that something has gone wrong in Walter's plan. Walter's fear forces him to deny the true purpose of Bobo's visit. Everything Walter says when Bobo first makes his entrance is an example of dramatic irony. While

Walter is asking Bobo to "tell him how things went in Springfield," the audience immediately guesses the outcome. Even the other characters on stage become aware of the impending doom long before Walter does. Walter arouses our pity when he asks Bobo, "There ain't nothin' wrong, is there?" Of course, something *is* wrong. But even as Bobo tries to tell him, Walter interrupts in order to rephrase his question, "Man—didn't nothin' go wrong?" Walter's dialouge continues in this vein until Bobo "hits him over the head" with the truth.

THEMATIC STRUCTURE

The underlying theme of Hansberry's *Raisin* is in the question posed by Langston Hughes' poem "Montage of a Dream Deferred," when he asks, "What happens to a dream deferred . . ." and then goes on to list the various things that might happen to a person if his dreams are put "on hold," emphasizing that whatever happens to a postponed dream is *never* good. More simply, the question Hansberry poses in her play is, "What happens to a person whose dreams grow more and more passionate—while his hopes of ever achieving those dreams grow dimmer each day?" Even the Bible concerns itself with this problem; in Proverbs 13:12, we read: "Hope deferred maketh the heart sick; but when the desire cometh, it is a tree of life." We see clearly what happens to Walter as his dream continues to be postponed by too many circumstances that are beyond his control.

Several other motifs are also successfully intertwined into this drama. Hansberry's avant-garde concerns, her prophetic political vision, and her ability to perceive the future importance of events that few people in 1959 were even aware of are used as lesser motifs or minor themes throughout the play.

The issue of **feminism** is one such example. Three generations of women reside in the Younger household, each possessing a different political perspective of herself as a woman. Mama (Lena Younger), in her early sixties, speaks "matter-of-factly" about her husband's prior womanizing. Ruth, about thirty, is more vocal about her feelings to her own husband than Mama was; still, Ruth is not as enlightened about a woman's "place" as is Beneatha, who is about twenty and pursuing a career that, in 1959, was largely a male-dominated profession.

Much of the conflict between Beneatha and Walter revolves

around Walter's chauvinistic view of Beneatha. When Walter complains that Beneatha's medical schooling will cost more than the family can afford, he bases his argument on the fact that since Beneatha is a woman, she should not even want to become a doctor. Walter's resentment and anger erupts in Act I, Scene 1: "Who in the hell told you you had to be a doctor? If you so crazy 'bout messing 'round with sick people — then go be a nurse like other women — or just get married and be quiet . . ."

Beneatha's defiance toward Walter is symbolic of her defiance toward all barriers of stereotype. She never yields to Walter and, in some cases, even goads him into a confrontation. Ruth's advice to Beneatha is that she should just "be nice" sometimes and not argue over every one of Walter's insensitive remarks. This advice is, of course, totally unacceptable to a character like Beneatha, to whom feistiness is a virtue and docility a "sin." Whereas Ruth tries to change herself in order to please everyone in her life, most especially to please her husband, Beneatha insists that others accept her as she is. She makes it clear, early on, that she has no use for George Murchison because of his shallow beliefs. She makes it clear to Ruth that she doesn't understand how anyone could have married someone like Walter. And she defies her mother on religious points; in fact, Mama has to slap Beneatha before she will back down. However, after Mama has left the room, Beneatha still says to Ruth that there is no God.

Mama is the "head of her household" only by default. She had to take charge after the death of Big Walter, whose name suggests that he was in charge of his family prior to his death. Mama appears to be always ready to hand over the reins to her son and let him be "head of the household" for one reason: he is a man. She entrusts Walter with the remaining insurance money because she feels that she has robbed him of his "manhood" by having done with the money what she thought was best. Mama is the type of woman who believes that the man should be in charge. Ruth apparently agrees, but Beneatha does not. Hansberry skillfully introduces issues of feminism that were not addressed as a political issue until a decade after the play's Broadway opening.

Along with feminism, the theme of **fecundity** (fertility, being fruitfully prolific) is threaded throughout this play. Three generations of Youngers live in the same household; in addition, both Ruth's possible pregnancy and her contemplation of abortion become focal points of the drama, and Mama's reference to the child that she lost is emphasized. She does not merely mention Baby Claude in conversation; rather she dwells upon her loss dramatically.

At the beginning of the play, Ruth serves eggs—but not without getting into an argument with Walter over the eggs—which again accentuates the importance of this symbol of fertility to the play. In addition, toward the end of the play, we learn that Mama's maiden name was Lena Eggleston, a name that underscores the theme of fecundity as much as the argument over eggs at the beginning of the play.

A related motif is the subject of **abortion,** which was taboo and illegal in 1959. Ruth considers an abortion in order to save her "living family" from further economic distress. The slightest reference to the word, however, sends the other family members into an emotional tailspin. Conflicts erupt between Mama and Walter, between Mama and Ruth, and between Ruth and Walter. Even Beneatha's inadvertently callous response to Ruth's pregnancy is "Where is it going to sleep? On the roof?" Other remarks are also proof that Beneatha's views on unplanned pregnancy differ sharply from her mother's. Mama says in exasperation: ". . . We [are] a people who give children life, not who destroys them . . ."; she would never agree to Ruth's having an abortion.

Ruth is trapped both by poverty and by the knowledge that her relationship with Walter Lee is rapidly deteriorating. Walter, although surprised to learn that she is contemplating an abortion, is still too caught up with his "get-rich-quick" scheme to offer her emotional support. Ruth contemplates an abortion because she believes this decision would be in the best interest of her family. Whether or not Ruth will actually decide on an abortion is debatable, for Ruth says to Mama in Act I, "Ain't nothin' can tear at you like losin' your baby." Ruth says this as Mama is recounting the pain of having lost her own baby, Claude. At this point in the play, Ruth's pregnancy has not yet been verified, but the dialogue spawned by the abortion controversy in this drama is as relevant today as it was in 1959, when the play opened.

Afrocentrism, or the expression of pride in one's African heritage, so popular among the black youth of the 1990s was, in 1959, a little-known phenomenon. But Lorraine Hansberry's affinity for all things African resulted from the people of greatness that she was acquainted with through her family. Langston Hughes, for example, was a friend of her father's and often came to the Hansberry home for dinner. Lorraine's uncle, Leo Hansberry, a noted historian and professor, was the teacher of Kwame Nkrumah while he was a student at Howard University. (Kwame Nkrumah was the leader of the fight for freedom of the Gold Coast from British rule and became its first president in 1957. The British name "Gold Coast" was changed to the Republic of Ghana in honor of that ancient kingdom.) Hansberry's knowledge and pride in her African heritage was a result of her family and her family's associations, something of which few other blacks could boast.

In this play, Beneatha expresses Hansberry's knowledge of and pride in her African heritage. Beneatha's Afrocentric spirit is nurtured by her relationship with the African, Asagai. Not only is Beneatha's dialogue peppered with a knowledge of 1959 African politics, but her dialogue also shows a knowledge of the ancient kingdoms of Africa, something few historians spoke of and even fewer people knew about.

In Act II, Scene 1, when Beneatha defines an "assimilationist Negro" as being ". . . someone who is willing to give up his own culture and submerge himself completely in the dominant . . . oppressive culture, . . ." George Murchison responds immediately with, "Here we go! A lecture on the African past! On our Great West African Heritage! In one second we will hear all about the great Ashanti empires; the great Songhay civilizations and the great sculpture of Benin and then some poetry in the Bantu. . . . Let's face it, baby, your heritage is nothing but a bunch of raggedy-assed spirituals and some grass huts."

In response to George's self-deprecating sarcasm about the historical achievements of black people, Beneatha screams at him from another room: ". . . the Ashanti were performing surgical operations when the English —were still tatooing themselves with blue dragons." It is clear that whatever George knows about Africa's past great civilizations has been learned through his association with Beneatha.

Note that when Beneatha's African suitor, Asagai, is on his way to the Younger apartment, Beneatha gives her mother a hasty briefing on African history, coaching her mother in conversational protocol. She tells Mama that Asagai is from Nigeria, which Mama immediately confuses with Liberia. After correcting her, Beneatha begs Mama not to make stereotypical comments about Africans and tells her that the only thing that most people seem to know about Africa has been learned from Tarzan movies. Beneatha berates those missionaries who, like Mama, are more concerned with changing the African's religion than in overthrowing colonial rule.

After Asagai arrives, Mama's attempt to impress him with her new knowledge of Africa is almost pathetic as she parrots what Beneatha has just told her, echoing Beneatha's previous dialogue almost verbatim. When *Raisin* opened in 1959, most people's knowledge of Africa was as limited as Mama's. Although a more enlightened modern audience might be chagrined by the political misconceptions of the late 50s, Lorraine Hansberry's prophetic vision is accurate and important, as though she envisioned the day that the true history of Africa would be widely known and that the shackles of colonialism would be broken. In 1959, when *Raisin* opened on Broadway, most African countries were under European rule. The following year, 1960, fifteen African countries gained their independence, and in eight more years, thirteen more had become independent.

In Act III, Beneatha and Asagai address the possibility of the African countries' replacing oppressive colonial rule with corrupt African leaders. Beneatha asks, "Independence and *then what?* What about the crooks and thieves and just plain idiots who will come into power and steal and plunder the same as before —only now they will be black and do it in the name of the new Independence . . ." Kwame Nkrumah received worldwide praise for his role in leading Ghana into independence in 1960.

However, immediately after taking office, Nkrumah began to spend the country's money with reckless abandon and embraced the Communist Party. The people rebelled against all of his dealings, staged a successful coup d'etat, and he was overthrown in 1966. In retrospect, Hansberry's prophetic accuracy is once again evident, for Nkrumah, in particular, was one of the leaders most admired by Hansberry in 1959, when *Raisin* opened. Other African nations also experienced political instability after their post–1959 independence.

Closely related to the theme of **Afrocentrism** in this play is Beneatha's decision to change her hairstyle. Although the dialogue concerning Beneatha's decision to change her hairstyle was omitted from the original stage presentation and from the original screenplay, this dialogue is in the complete, original version of the play and was used in the 1989 American Playhouse TV presentation.

In Act I, Scene 2, Asagai's off-hand remark about Beneatha's straightened hair is the catalyst for her dramatic change in Act II, Scene 1 (ironically, for her date with George Murchison and not for a date with Asagai). In Act I, Scene 2, when Asagai presents Beneatha with Nigerian tribal robes, he says, "You wear it well . . . mutilated hair and all." His meaning is clear, although Beneatha's sensitivity does not permit her to immediately grasp his meaning. So Asagai explains by asking, "Were you born with it [your hair] like that?"

In Act II, Scene 1, Beneatha was supposed to have come out for her date with a natural (unstraightened) hairstyle; this scene, however, was omitted at the last minute from the original stage presentation because the actress, Diana Sands, in the role of Beneatha, received an imperfect haircut. Since this would have given a negative impression of the natural look, both Hansberry and Sands decided to omit the hairstyle change from the Broadway opening. It is interesting to note that in 1959, Beneatha's new hairstyle would have sent some shock waves throughout the audience, whereas ten years later, the same style had become so popular nationwide that it was promoted by Madison Avenue as the "Afro." Once again, Hansberry's prophetic vision was accurate and on target.

Throughout *Raisin,* Hansberry expresses her own desire to see blacks in entrepreneurial ventures. So few blacks were in business in 1959 that sociologists of that day addressed this concern in academic publications. Mama says, in response to Ruth's echoing Walter's dream of owning his own business, "We ain't no business people, Ruth. We just plain working folks," and Ruth answers with: "Ain't nobody business people till they go into business. Walter Lee says colored people ain't never going to start getting ahead till they start gambling on some different kinds of things in the world—investments and things." Because the percentage of black people who own their own businesses has increased dramatically since 1959, one might conclude that, here once again, Hansberry had an accurate view of the future.

LANGUAGE AND STYLE

Clearly, Lorraine Hansberry understood that the dialects of black communities were distinctly different from the dialects of other communities, for she has her characters speak in the very *real* language of their community. Although Hansberry's own immediate family were all college educated and spoke Standard English all the time at home, Hansberry herself spent a lot of time in poor Southside households that were similar to that of the Younger family in *Raisin*. Naturally Mama's speech is different from Beneatha's; however, there are even subtle differences between the speech patterns of Mama and Walter and Ruth and Bobo.

The language of many of the characters of *Raisin* is unconventially non-Standard English; the black characters are not merely speaking English that is ungrammatical, a characteristic of the unlearned; rather, they are speaking a dialect common in the black communities that are heavily populated by migrants from the South. Their dialect, although similar to the white southern dialect, is distinctly different in that it is mostly an outgrowth of the period of slavery. At that time slaves were forbidden a formal education and therefore mimicked whatever English they heard, ending up with a "Pidgin English" not unlike the English spoken by many of the Native American population.

It is natural to superimpose one's known grammatical structure upon a language that one is attempting to learn, as in the German placement of the direct object *after* any interrupting phrase; it was comically noted at the turn of the century that the recent German immigrants would readily construct the following type of English sentence: Throw Mama from the stairs her hat. In the same way, the slaves, many of whom were from West Africa, superimposed their own grammatical structure upon their new master's language, ending up with what linguists define today as "Black English." Broadly explained, Black English has its own grammatical structure — even though it is non-Standard English. It is not solely "bad grammar," for in *some* cases, the "errors" are intentional for effect.

The most prominent example of this dialect is in the "abuse" of the verb "to be." Blacks have always "abused" the grammatical form of the verb "to be" in *whatever* language slaves were forced to learn — be it English, French, Spanish, or Dutch. These "abuses" are even found in Surinam, which proves the result of the African continuum, for many West African languages have a habitual tense which translates as "to be." Note the following examples of this habitual tense:

(1) Harry be waiting for me every night when I come home.

(2) You can never reach Mary because she be talking on the phone.

(3) Donald be so tired when he leaves work.

In each of the above examples, the word "be" means "all of the time."

However, in the following examples, forms of the verb "to be" are purposely omitted in order to express a different meaning:

(1) The answer to the question: "What is Harry doing right now?" might be, "He waiting."

(2) The answer to the question: "What is Mary doing right now?" might be, "She talking on the phone."

Note that in the above examples, there are distinctly different meanings. When the word "be" is used in the above constructions, the meaning is "all the time." Omitting the main verb before the participle means the action is taking place "right now." So, in the black dialect, "He talking" means something completely different from "He be talking."

Hansberry had to have been aware of the semantic subtleties of the black dialect in order to have made these points in *Raisin*.

Note the following examples from various scenes of *Raisin*.

Walter: I can't be bein' late to work on account of him fooling around in there.

Ruth: Oh, no he ain't going to be getting up no earlier no such thing!

Ruth: Walter, don't be dragging me in it.

Also in the black dialect, one moves directly from the subject to its adjective, getting to the point more quickly by having eliminated any forms of the verb "to be." For example, one might hear someone say in black dialect, "Don't bother Lisa 'cause she tired." One might also hear "She pretty," "He ugly," "They smart," etc.

Note the following from various scenes in *Raisin*:

Walter: You tired, ain't you? Tired of everything ...

Walter: We one group of men tied to a race of women with small minds ...

Mama: But [Beneatha] you so thin ...

Mama: We ain't no business people, Ruth. We just plain working folks.

> *Mama:* Ruth honey—what's the matter with you—you sick?
>
> *Ruth:* You think you a woman, Bennie—but you still a little girl.

In the black dialect, the word **done** means something completely different from the Standard English past participle of the verb "to do." Note the following examples:

(1) It's too late to ask her 'cause she **done** gone.
(2) Mrs. Jackson **done** burned the cabbage again.
(3) I **done** told you—I didn't do it!

In the above examples, **done** means **has already** or **have already**. Note the following examples from *Raisin:*

> *Ruth:* You done spoiled that boy so . . .
>
> *Mama:* What done got into you, girl? Walter Lee done finally sold you on investing?
>
> *Mama:* And all that money they pour into these churches when they ought to be helping you people over there drive out them French and Englishmen done taken away your land.
>
> *Mama:* Much baking powder as she done borrowed from me all these years, she could of done gone into the baking business.
>
> *Mama:* [The check] . . . you mean it really done come?
>
> *Ruth:* Girl, you done lost your natural mind?

Another intentional Standard English deviation is the overuse of the negative in order to emphasize that negative, as in the following: "Nobody ain't never seen no ghost nowhere."

In *Raisin,* this construction abounds as in the following examples taken from various scenes:

> *Mama:* Now here come you and Beneatha talking 'bout things we ain't never even thought about hardly . . .
>
> *Mama:* I'm waiting to see you stand up and . . . say we done give up one baby to poverty and that we ain't going to give up nary another one . . .
>
> *Bobo:* Willy didn't never show up . . .
>
> *Ruth:* Walter, that ain't none of our money . . .

In addition to the obvious lack of formal education noted in Mama's speech, her speech is also flavored with "southernisms," which are absent from Walter's speech. Even though Walter does not have as much education as Beneatha, he is not as unschooled as Mama, nor does he use the southernisms that define Mama. Ruth, however, proves through her speech, that she has not had even as much formal education as Walter, for her speech is as flavored with southernisms as Mama's. Because Ruth makes far more Standard English errors than Walter does, her speech makes her sound as though she is older than her thirty years. Ruth sounds more like Mama than any of the other characters in the play. The neighbor, Mrs. Johnson, proves that her roots are also southern by her speech, and Bobo also reveals his obvious southern upbringing when he speaks to Ruth, and is overly polite in deference to her gender:

Bobo:	Well, **h'you, Miss** Ruth.
Mrs. Johnson:	I finds I can't close my eyes right **lessen I done had** that last cup of coffee . . .
Mama:	My children and **they** tempers . . .
Ruth:	If you don't take this comb and fix [your hair], **you better!**
Mama:	**Who that** 'round here slamming doors at this hour?
Mama:	This all the packing **got done** since I **left out of here** this morning—I **testify before God** . . .
Mama:	Tell that **youngun** to get himself up here . . .

The luxuriousness of Hansberry's writing is apparent in her scene descriptions prior to Act I. An example of ordinary writing might be "The room was overcrowded with old, outdated furniture." Note, as a contrast, Hansberry's more poetic way of saying the same thing: "The Younger living room would be a comfortable and well-ordered room if it were not for a number of indestructible contradictions to this state of being. Its furnishings are typical and undistinguished and their primary feature now is that they have clearly had to accommodate the living of too many people for too many years — and they are tired."

As another example, ordinary writing might be: The furnishings of this room used to be beautiful, but are now faded, ugly and even tasteless." Hansberry, however, says it this way: "Still, we can see that at some time, a time probably no longer remembered by the family (except perhaps for Mama), the furnishings of this room were actually selected with care and love and even hope — and brought to this apartment and arranged with taste and pride. That was a long time ago. Now the once loved pattern of the couch upholstery has to fight to show itself from under acres of crocheted doilies and couch covers which have themselves finally come to be more important than the upholstery."

An ordinary way of describing the worn out carpet might be to say: "Although they tried, they could not hide the worn out look of the old carpet . . ." Now, note Hansberry's description: "And here a table or a chair has been moved to disguise the worn places in the carpet; but the carpet has fought back by showing its weariness, with depressing uniformity, elsewhere on its surface."

So too, this example: Ordinary: "Everything in this room looks old and unattractive." In contrast, Hansberry: "Weariness has, in fact, won in this room. Everything has been polished, washed, sat on, used, scrubbed too often. All pretenses but living itself have long since vanished from the very atmosphere of this room."

THREE VERSIONS OF *A RAISIN IN THE SUN*

Original Stage Play, Original Screenplay, and the American Playhouse Presentation

The complete, original version of Hansberry's play includes several scenes with which most people are not familiar, for these were omitted from the original stage presentations of *Raisin* when it opened in 1959. Most of the cuts from the complete version were made because of time constraints.

For example, the entire scene with Mrs. Johnson was eliminated from the original stage presentation of *Raisin*. Another deletion from the complete version was the scene in which Beneatha has cut her hair and is wearing it in the "natural" style that she knows Asagai will admire.

This scene, although very important to Hansberry, was taken out because, just before the show opened, the actress playing the role of Beneatha had inadvertently been given a disastrous haircut, which everyone involved in the production of *Raisin* felt would have made a negative statement to the audience about Hansberry's true, positive feelings about the natural hairstyle. The dramatic change in Beneatha's hairstyle is shown in the complete version, the American Playhouse television presentation.

Another omission from the original stage production, but one which appears in the complete version (and in the American Playhouse presentation) is in the scene in which Travis is playing with a group of neighborhood boys; for sport, they are chasing a rat. Later, Travis is at home, telling his family about the fun he had chasing the rat with his friends.

In each of these scenes which were omitted from the original stage production, Hansberry was attempting to make a deeply felt statement. In the scene with Mrs. Johnson, Hansberry takes a position on the Booker T. Washington/W. E. B. Du Bois debate, in which Hansberry is clearly siding with Du Bois. Hansberry is also using this scene to poke fun at the blacks who are too fearful of racist reprisals to demand equality.

In the scene where Beneatha unveils the natural look, Hansberry is making a statement on the identity crisis within the black community long before the Afrocentric awakening of the 90s.

In the scene where Travis is chasing a rat for sport, Hansberry is attempting to show the horrors that daily confront the children of the poor.

The screenplay of *Raisin* (the film was released in 1960) is altered in many ways. In Act I, Scene 1, Walter Lee gives Travis a dollar (that he can ill afford). In the complete version and in the American Playhouse presentation, Walter Lee returns to ask Ruth for fifty cents for carfare to work. This is omitted from the screenplay. In the screenplay, not only does Walter not return, but he is later seen at his job as a chauffeur. In this scene in the screenplay, Walter is standing near his boss' limousine in a heavily populated metropolitan area. In the stage presentation and even in the complete version (which includes the American Playhouse presentation), Walter talks about going to the Green Hat, a bar that he frequents, but the screenplay version has Mama going to the bar in order to find Walter. In the screenplay, Mama goes to the Green Hat and gives Walter the $6,500 *in the bar*.

The screenplay also shows the Younger family actually going to their new house in Clybourne Park. Neither the original stage production nor the complete version nor the American Playhouse presentation shows the Younger family in any setting other than their Southside apartment.

A Raisin in the Sun was revised as the musical *Raisin* and ran on Broadway from October 1973 until December 1975 for 847 performances. It won the Tony and Grammy Awards as Best Musical, and it toured 50 cities. *Raisin* was so well received that the mayors of the cities and the governors of the states in which it toured often proclaimed the show's arrival as "Lorraine Hansberry Day."

BIOGRAPHICAL SKETCHES OF ORIGINAL CAST

Ruth Younger	**Ruby Dee**
Travis Younger	**Glynn Turman**
Walter Lee Younger ("Brother")	**Sidney Poitier**
Beneatha Younger	**Diana Sands**
Mama	**Claudia McNeil**
Joseph Asagai	**Ivan Dixon**
George Murchison	**Louis Gossett**
Karl Lindner	**John Fiedler**
Bobo	**Lonne Elder III**
Moving Men	**Ed Hall, Douglas Turner**
Directed by	**Lloyd Richards**

Some of the above actors went on to make their marks in the American theater while others of this group made a lasting impression in Hollywood. All the members of the original cast of *A Raisin in the Sun* became successful actors, although nearly all of them were unknown when the play opened in 1959.

Ruby Dee (Ruth), the wife of veteran actor **Ossie Davis,** has received critical acclaim for her many stage performances and has appeared in numerous films, including Spike Lee's *Do The Right Thing,* for which she received an Academy Award nomination for Best Supporting Actress.

Glynn Turman (Travis) has appeared in numerous Hollywood films and, as of this writing, he appears in the weekly television series *A Different World,* as the on-campus military presence.

Sidney Poitier (Walter Lee) has appeared in numerous Hollywood films, receiving an Academy Award for his performance in *Lilies Of The Field,* in 1963.

Diana Sands (Beneatha) continued her stellar performances in the legitimate theater until her untimely death at age 39 in 1973. Although she was not known as a Hollywood actress, Sands, just prior to her death, was scheduled for the female lead with James Earl Jones in the movie *Claudine,* a role that ultimately went to Diahann Carroll.

By the time **Claudia McNeil** (Mama) had been chosen as the matriarch of the Younger family in *Raisin,* she had already appeared in Langston Hughes' *Simply Heavenly* in 1957 and in *Winesburg, Ohio* in 1958. Avoiding Hollywood, she continued her work as a stage actress, where she remained a beacon for aspirants to the legitimate theater.

After appearing in *Wedding in Japan* in 1957 and in *Cave Dwellers* the same year, **Ivan Dixon** (Joseph Asagai) landed his role on stage in *Raisin* in 1959. Since then, he has appeared in numerous Hollywood films and is perhaps best known for his television role as one of *Hogan's Heroes,* the popular 60s sitcom.

Louis Gossett, Jr. (George Murchison) has appeared in numerous Hollywood films, receiving the Academy Award for Best Supporting Actor in *An Officer and a Gentleman* in 1982. However, he is best known for his portrayal of "Fiddler" in Alex Haley's television miniseries, *Roots.*

John Fiedler (Karl Lindner) has enjoyed a lengthy and well-earned reputation as one of this country's great character actors, appearing in numerous films such as *Billy Budd,* 1945; *The Odd Couple,* 1965; and *Our Town,* 1969.

After his appearance in *Raisin* in 1959, **Lonne Elder III** (Bobo) joined the Negro Ensemble Company, a theater company founded by Douglas Turner Ward, one of the moving men in the original stage production of *Raisin.* In 1965, Lonne Elder appeared in *Day of Absence,* a very successful Negro Ensemble Company production. Then, in 1967, Lonne Elder's venture into the realm of playwrighting proved successful when he penned the award-winning *Ceremonies in Dark Old Men.*

Douglas Turner Ward (Moving Man) founded the Negro Ensemble Company in 1967 with Robert Hooks. A director and actor, he is also well known for his two plays *Day of Absence* and *Happy Ending.*

Lloyd Richards, the Director of *Raisin* was named Dean of the Yale Drama School in 1979.

SUGGESTED ESSAY QUESTIONS

(1) In literature, as in life, a character may search for a better way of life. Show how *two* characters from *A Raisin in the Sun* are searching for a better way of life. Explain what each character is hoping to gain through this search and discuss the ways in which each character attempts to bring about a change in his or her life.

(2) Discuss the ways in which the setting of *Raisin* has a profound effect upon two of the characters.

(3) If people can be divided into three groups—those who make things happen, those who watch things happen, and those who wonder what happened—apply each of these to the three characters in *Raisin* who respectively prove that this is so.

(4) Often, pressure from other people or from outside forces might compel a person to take an action that he or she might not have taken ordinarily. Discuss a character from *Raisin* who was pressured into taking an action that he or she might not have taken on his or her own.

(5) Show how *Raisin* deals with the generation gap—the problems that the older generation have in dealing with the younger generation and vice versa.

(6) Discuss the ways in which two characters in *Raisin* have made adjustments to negative aspects of their environment. These adjustments might be to the character's physical surroundings, to other people, or to the customs and traditions of the society in which they live.

(7) Sometimes something as seemingly trivial as a meeting or a conversation between two people can have a lasting effect upon the life of one or even of both of them. Discuss how either a seemingly unimportant meeting or a casual conversation brings about a significant change in the life of one of the characters in *Raisin*.

(8) Sometimes in one work of literature, we might find two characters who contrast markedly from one another. Discuss two

characters from *Raisin* who are the opposite of each other in their views, beliefs, and philosophy of life.

(9) In literature, as in life, a character might feel trapped. Discuss a character from *Raisin* who feels trapped and give examples of the ways in which this character chooses to deal with those feelings.

(10) Discuss a character from *Raisin* who changes significantly, telling specifically of the forces that bring about this change. How does this character relate to the other characters before the change and how does this character relate to the other characters after the change?

(11) Most people define loneliness as being alone, but a person might experience loneliness even when surrounded by other people. A person can be lonely if his/her ideas, feelings, or circumstances are different from those around them. Discuss a character from *Raisin* who experiences loneliness because of the differences in his/her ideas, feelings, or circumstances.

(12) Often, in life, a situation may reach a "point of no return" — the point after which the life of a person can never be the same. Describe such a turning point for a character in *Raisin*.

(13) Add another ending to the already existing ending of *Raisin*. Describe what you think happens next — after the Youngers have left their Southside Chicago apartment and have moved into their new house. You might write a composition or you may wish to continue in Hansberry's genre, using the dialogue of the characters to show your plot.

(14) Noting Lorraine Hansberry's unique writing style, compare Walter Lee's imitation of a subservient, stereotypical begging "darky," (the heartbreaking speech he plans to deliver to Lindner in order to regain the lost money) with the speech that Walter Lee actually gives when Lindner arrives. How are they different in language? What is Hansberry's point in having Walter Lee practice one speech and then say something completely different?

RELATED RESEARCH PROJECTS

(1) After reading a full-length biography of Langston Hughes, show how he might have had a profound effect on Lorraine Hansberry's writing of *A Raisin in the Sun.*

(2) After reading a full-length biography of Lorraine Hansberry, discuss the ways in which events of her own life are interwoven into her play *A Raisin in the Sun.*

(3) Research the following events of 1955 and tell how each might have contributed to Lorraine Hansberry's political philosophy:
• The arrest of Rosa Parks.
• Brown v. Board of Education of Topeka.
• The murder of Emmett Till.

(4) In order to be more aware of the historical events surrounding the opening of Raisin on Broadway, summarize the headlines of *The New York Times* for March 11, 1959 (the date Raisin opened on Broadway); also summarize a full-length article from *Life* magazine for that week; and summarize an article from *Ebony* magazine for that month.

SELECTED BIBLIOGRAPHY

ATKINSON, BROOKS. "*A Raisin in the Sun.*" *New York Times* 12 March 1959.

BALDWIN, JAMES. "Sweet Lorraine." *Esquire* November 1969: 139–40.

BELASCO, MILTON JAY, and HAROLD E. HAMMOND. *Africa.* New York: Globe, 1981.

BOND, JEAN CAREY. "The Triumphs of Lorraine Hansberry." *Philadelphia Tribune* 18 May 1979: 4–6.

BROOKS, LESTER. *Great Civilizations of Ancient Africa.* New York: Four Winds Press, 1971.

CHU, DANIEL, and ELLIOT SKINNER. *A Glorious Age in Africa*. New York: Doubleday, 1965.

CROWDER, CHARLES. *Africa*. Regions of Our World. New York: William H. Sadlier, 1974.

DAVIDSON, BASIL. *The African Slave Trade*. Boston: Little, Brown & Co., 1961.

_____. *A History of West Africa to the Nineteenth Century*. New York: Doubleday, 1966.

DA SILVA, BENJAMIN, et. al. *The Afro American in United States History*. New York: Globe, 1969.

DAVIS, OSSIE. "The Significance of Lorraine Hansberry." *Freedomways* 5.3 (Summer 1965): 396–402.

DILLARD, J. L. *Black English*. 1972. New York: Vintage Paperback, 1973.

DIOP, CHEIKH ANTA. *Precolonial Black Africa*. New York: Lawrence Hill Books, 1987.

FARRELL, WILLIAM E. "600 Attend Hansberry Rites; Paul Robeson Delivers Eulogy." *New York Times* 17 January 1965.

GAYLE, ADDISON, ed. *The Black Aesthetic*. 1971. New York: Anchor Books, 1972.

GOTTLIEB, DANIEL W. "*A Raisin in the Sun* Premieres at Shubert." *Hartford Times* 22 January 1959. *Raisin's* successful opening at Hartford's Shubert Theater in January 1959 led to its Broadway opening in New York in March at the Ethel Barrymore Theater. Hansberry's own comment on Gottlieb's review: "One reviewer who really understood the play . . . "

HANSBERRY, LORRAINE. *A Raisin in the Sun*. 1958. New York: Penguin, 1959. The complete original version.

——————————. *To Be Young, Gifted and Black: Lorraine Hansberry in Her Own Words*. Foreword by Robert Nemiroff. 1969. New York: New American Library, 1970. Biography drawn from letters, journals, essays, memoirs, poetry, and dramatic scenes.

——————————. "Letter to the Editor." *Time* 7 February 1964. Regards *Time* magazine's previous article on the commercial exploitation of sex in America.

HARRISON, PAUL CARTER. *The Drama of Nommo*. New York: Grove Press, 1972.

HASKINS, JAMES, and HUGH F. BUTTS, M. D. *The Psychology of Black Language*. New York: Barnes and Noble Books, Harper and Row, 1973.

HAYS, PETER L. "*Raisin in the Sun* and *Juno and the Peacock*." *Phylon* 33 (1972): 175–76.

KEYSSAR-FRANKE, HELENE. "Afro-American Drama and Its Criticism, 1960–1972: An Annotated Check List with Appendices." *Bulletin of the New York Public Library* 78.3 (Spring 1975): 324–26.

KHAMIT-KUSH, INDUS. *What They Never Told*. New York: Luxorr Publications, 1983.

LINDSAY, JOHN V. "Remarks in the House of Representatives on the Death of Lorraine Hansberry and Insertions from the *New York Herald Tribune*, January 13, 1965." *Congressional Record*. U.S. 89th Cong., 1st sess. 1965.

"Lorraine Hansberry on Negro Writers." *New York Herald Tribune* 2 March 1959. Excerpts from her speech at the First Conference of Negro Writers, New York City, February 28–March 28, 1959.

"Lorraine Hansberry, 34, Dies; Author of *A Raisin in the Sun*." Obituary. *New York Times* 13 January 1965.

MAJOR, CLARENCE. *Dictionary of Afro-American Slang*. New York: International Publishers (New World Paperbacks), 1970.

MILLER, JEANE-MARIE. "Images of Black Women in Plays by Black Playwrights." *CLA Journal* 20.4 (June 1977): 494–507.

NEMIROFF, ROBERT. *To Be Young, Gifted and Black*. Drama. New York: Samuel French, 1971. This play should not be confused with the full-length, autobiographical work from which it is adapted, and which carries the same title.

NEMIROFF, ROBERT, and LORRAINE HANSBERRY. "Amen." *Village Voice* 25 March 1959: 4. A Letter to the Editor regarding the South African Defense Fund.

NEMIROFF, ROBERT, and CHARLOTTE ZALTBERG. *Raisin*. Broadway Musical. New York: Columbia Records, 1973. Columbia KS 32754.

OSEI, G. K. *The African*. New York: University Books, 1971.

A Raisin in the Sun. Dir. Daniel Petrie. 1961.

ROBINSON, LAYHMOND. "Robert Kennedy Consults Negroes Here About the North." *New York Times* 25 May 1963: 1, 8. Meeting with Baldwin, Hansberry, Belafonte, et. al.

——————————. "Robert Kennedy Fails to Sway Negroes at Secret Talks Here." *New York Times* 26 May 1963: 1, 59.

ROGERS, J. A. *Africa's Gift to America*. New York: Helga Rogers, 1961.

WALKER, ALICE. "One Child of One's Own." *Ms.* (August 1979): 72–73.

WHITE, E. B. "Talk of the Town: Playwright." *New Yorker* 9 May 1959: 33–35. Interview with Lorraine Hansberry.